EASY SOFTWARE ENGINEERING

AN ESSENTIAL GUIDE

RANJOT SINGH

XpressPublishing
An imprint of Notion Press

XpressPublishing
An imprint of Notion Press

Old No. 38, New No. 6
McNichols Road, Chetpet
Chennai - 600 031

First Published by Notion Press 2019
Copyright © Ranjot Singh 2019
All Rights Reserved.

ISBN 978-1-64828-247-8

To begin with, I would like to thank the Almighty for giving me the intellect to create this book.Many authors have contributed to creating this priceless guide. Words are not enough to explain how thankful i am to those who have joined me on this journey. In my Final year of Bachelor of Computer Application, I realised there was a lack of books which simply explained Software Engineering. This is what inspired me to write an easy accessible book for fellow students and future students .

Ranjot Singh

Ranjotsinghchahal@gmail.com

E-book Publisher : RANA BOOKS INDIA

Contents

Contents

Preface

One thing which students find frustrating about Software Engineering is understanding the complex language used in textbooks. Not many textbooks are user-friendly, which in turn, frustrates students. The author, Ranjot Singh, aimed to change this by creating a textbook using easy-to-understand language. This allows you to enjoy the learning process, as well as digest the information with ease.

This book is ideal for students from Punjabi University Patiala studying the Bachelor of Computer Applications, however, it can be useful for anyone with an interest in Software Engineering. It begins with basic information regarding the paper ie. Lecture duration, paper duration and structure of the paper. Section A begins introducing The Problem Domain, Software engineering challenges and Software engineering approach. Section B outlines Software design, coding, testing and software maintenance.

I hope you enjoy reading this book as much as I enjoyed writing it. Wishing you all the best in your studies.

Ranjot Singh

About Writer

Ranjot Singh

Ranjot Singh, also known by the name Jot Chahal, has wrote many books which he has recently published. As well as writing, Chahal is also a Third-Year student in BCA (Degree name)from Punjabi University Patiala Baba Jogi Peer Neighbourhood Campus, Ralla He belongs to Mansa district of Punjab. His books contains many poetry and quotes which reflects his thoughts and touches the reader's heart. His most recent book, The Perfect Life (100+ Positive thoughts for your life): Everything in your hands. His books are mainly in English, Hindi and Punjabi.

Syllabus

BCA-324: Software Engineering

Max Marks: 75   Maximum Time: 3 Hrs Min Pass Marks: 35%   Lectures to be delivered: 45-55 Hrs

(A) INSTRUCTION FOR THE PAPER SETTER The question paper will consist of three sections A, B and C. Section A and B will have four questions from the respective section of the syllabus carrying 15 marks for each question. Section C will consist of 5-10 short answer type questions carrying a total of 15 marks, which will cover the entire syllabus uniformly. . Candidates are required to attempt five questions in all by selecting at least two questions each from the section A and B. Section C is compulsory.

SECTION – A Introduction – The Problem Domain, Software Engg.Challenges, Software Engg.Approach. Software development life cycle, its phases, Software development process models :Waterfall, Prototyping, Iterative; Software Process- Characteristics of software process, Project management process, Software configuration management process. Project Planning – activities, COCOMO model.Software Metrics – Definition, Importance, Categories of metrics. Software Quality – Attributes,Cyclomatic complexity metric. Software Requirements Analysis – Need for SRS, Data flow diagrams, Data Dictionary, entity relationship diagram, Characteristics and components of SRS, validation, metrics

SECTION-B Software Design – Design principles, Module-level concepts, Structure Chart and Structured Design methodology,, verification, metrics : network metrics, information flow metrics. Coding – Programming Principles and Guidelines, Verification- code inspections, static analysis.Software Testing – testing fundamentals, Black Box Testing : Equivalence class partitioning, Boundary value analysis, cause-effect graphing; White Box Testing : Control flow and Data flow based testing, mutation testing; levels of testing, test plan, test case specification, test case execution and analysis, Software maintenance – Categories of maintenance.Software Reliability – Definition, uses of reliability studies

CHAPTER ONE

INTRODUCTION

Software is a program or set of programs containing instructions which provide desired functionality . And Engineering is the processes of designing and building something that serves a particular purpose and find a cost effective solution to problems.

Software Engineering is a systematic approach to the design, development, operation, and maintenance of a software system.

Dual Role of Software:

1.As a product –

- It delivers the computing potential across network of Hardware.
- It enables the Hardware to deliver the expected functionality.
- It acts as information transformer because it produces, manages, acquires, modifies, displays, or transmits information.

2.As a vehicle for delivering a product –

- It provides system functionality (e.g., payroll system)
- It controls other software (e.g., an operating system)
- It helps build other software (e.g., software tools)

Objectives of Software Engineering:

Maintainability –

It should be feasible for the software to evolve to meet changing requirements.

Correctness –

A software product is correct, if the different requirements as specified in the SRS document have been correctly implemented.

Reusability –

A software product has good reusability, if the different modules of the product can easily be reused to develop new products.

Testability –

Here software facilitates both the establishment of test criteria and the evaluation of the software with respect to those criteria.

Reliability –

It is an attribute of software quality. The extent to which a program can be expected to perform its desired function, over an arbitrary time period.

Portability –

In this case, software can be transferred from one computer system or environment to another.

Adaptability –

In this case, software allows differing system constraints and user needs to be satisfied by making changes to the software.

Program vs Software Product:

- Program is a set of instruction related each other where as Software Product is a collection of program designed for specific task.
- Programs are usually small in size where as Software Products are usually large in size.
- Programs are developed by individuals that means single user where as Software Product are developed by large no of users.
- In program, there is no documentation or lack in proper documentation.
- In Software Product, Proper documentation and well documented and user manual prepared.
- Development of program is Unplanned, not Systematic etc but Development of Software Product is well Systematic, organised, planned approach.
- Programs provide Limited functionality and less features where as Software Products provides more functionality as they are big in size (lines of codes) more options and features.
- **The importance of Software engineering is as follows:**

1. Reduces complexity: Big software is always complicated and challenging to progress. Software engineering has a great solution to reduce the complication of any project. Software engineering divides big problems into various small issues. And then start solving each small issue one by

one. All these small problems are solved independently to each other.

2. To minimize software cost: Software needs a lot of hardwork and software engineers are highly paid experts. A lot of manpower is required to develop software with a large number of codes. But in software engineering, programmers project everything and decrease all those things that are not needed. In turn, the cost for software productions becomes less as compared to any software that does not use software engineering method.

3. To decrease time: Anything that is not made according to the project always wastes time. And if you are making great software, then you may need to run many codes to get the definitive running code. This is a very time-consuming procedure, and if it is not well handled, then this can take a lot of time. So if you are making your software according to the software engineering method, then it will decrease a lot of time.

4. Handling big projects: Big projects are not done in a couple of days, and they need lots of patience, planning, and management. And to invest six and seven months of any company, it requires heaps of planning, direction, testing, and maintenance. No one can say that he has given four months of a company to the task, and the project is still in its first stage. Because the company has provided many resources to the plan and it should be completed. So to handle a big project without any problem, the company has to go for a software engineering method.

5. Reliable software: Software should be secure, means if you have delivered the software, then it should work for at least its given time or subscription. And if any bugs come in the software, the company is responsible for solving all these bugs. Because in software engineering, testing and maintenance are given, so there is no worry of its reliability.

6. Effectiveness: Effectiveness comes if anything has made according to the standards. Software standards are the big target of companies to make it more effective. So Software becomes more effective in the act with the help of software engineering.

Classification of Software

The software is used extensively in several domains including hospitals, banks, schools, defence, finance, stock markets and so on. It can be categorized into different types:

On the basis of application:

System Software –

System Software is necessary to manage the computer resources and support the execution of application programs. Software like operating systems, compilers, editors and drivers etc., come under this category. A computer cannot function without the presence of these. Operating systems are needed to link the machine dependent needs of a program with the capabilities of the machine on which it runs. Compilers translate programs from high-level language to machine language.

Networking and Web Applications Software –

Networking Software provides the required support necessary for computers to interact with each other and with data storage facilities. The networking software is also used when software is running on a network of computers (such as World Wide Web). It includes all network management software, server software, security and encryption software and software to develop web-based applications like HTML, PHP, XML, etc.

Embedded Software –

This type of software is embedded into the hardware normally in the Read Only Memory (ROM) as a part of a large system and is used to support certain functionality under the control conditions. Examples are software used in instrumentation and control applications, washing machines, satellites, microwaves, washing machines etc.

Reservation Software –

A Reservation system is primarily used to store and retrieve information and perform transactions related to air travel, car rental, hotels, or other activities. They also provide access to bus and railway reservations, although these are not always integrated with the main system. These are also used to relay computerized information for users in the hotel industry, making a reservation and ensuring that the hotel is not overbooked.

Business Software –

This category of software is used to support the business applications and is the most widely used category of software. Examples are software for inventory management, accounts, banking, hospitals, schools, stock markets, etc.

Entertainment Software –

Education and entertainment software provides a powerful tool for educational agencies, especially those that deal with educating young children. There is a wide range of entertainment software such as computer games, educational games, translation software, mapping software, etc.

Artificial Intelligence Software –

Software like expert systems, decision support systems, pattern recognition software, artificial neural networks, etc. come under this category. They involve complex problems which are not affected by complex computations using non-numerical algorithms.

Scientific Software –

Scientific and engineering software satisfies the needs of a scientific or engineering user to perform enterprise specific tasks. Such software is written for specific applications using principles, techniques and formulae specific to that field. Examples are software like MATLAB, AUTOCAD, PSPICE, ORCAD, etc.

Utilities Software –

The programs coming under this category perform specific tasks and are different from other software in terms of size, cost and complexity. Examples are anti-virus software, voice recognition software, compression programs, etc.

Document Management Software –

A Document Management Software is used to track, manage and store documents in order to reduce the paperwork. Such systems are capable of keeping a record of the various versions created and modified by different users (history tracking). They commonly provide storage, versioning, metadata, security, as well as indexing and retrieval capabilities.

On the basis of copyright:

Commercial –

It represents the majority of software which we purchase from software companies, commercial computer stores, etc. In this case, when a user buys a software, they acquire a license key to use it. Users are not allowed to make the copies of the software. The copyright of the program is owned by the company.

Shareware –

Shareware software is also covered under copyright but the purchasers are allowed to make and distribute copies with the condition that after testing the software, if the purchaser adopts it for use, then they must pay for it.

In both of the above types of software, changes to software are not allowed.

Freeware –
In general, according to freeware software licenses, copies of the software can be made both for archival and distribution purposes but here, distribution cannot be for making a profit. Derivative works and modifications to the software are allowed and encouraged. Decompiling of the program code is also allowed without the explicit permission of the copyright holder.

Public Domain –
In case of public domain software, the original copyright holder explicitly relinquishes all rights to the software. Hence software copies can be made both for archival and distribution purposes with no restrictions on distribution. Modifications to the software and reverse engineering are also allowed.

Problem Domain:

Problem domain (or **problem space**) is an engineering term referring to all information that defines the problem and constrains the solution (the constraints being part of the problem). It includes the goals that the problem owner wishes to achieve, the context within which the problem exists, and all rules that define essential functions or other aspects of any solution product. It represents the environment in which a solution will have to operate, as well as the problem itself.

It is called scope of analysis, When collecting user stories or User Requirements whatever, how do you decide which ones are relevant? You keep in mind some higher-level statement of what the objectives are and what people think the problems are (if people didn't think there were problems, they wouldn't be paying someone to come up with a solution, would they?). Then it's either in, out or borderline. If it's borderline, you probably want someone to agree it's out (even if you want it to be in). In the mean time, and probably afterwards, you keep it as Something to think about.

Note that the customer for a software solution (the "problem owner") doesn't necessarily recognise the existence of a problem so much as an opportunity. An engineer sees a "problem domain" as being the set of circumstances for which s/he has to provide a solution; it's the engineer's problem, not necessarily the customer's.

Solution Domain:

While the Problem Domain defines the environment where the solution will come to work, the solution domain defines the abstract environment where the solution is developed. The differences between those two domains are the cause for possible errors when the solution is planted into the problem domain.

In respect to a given problem (or set of problems), the **solution domain** (or **solution space**) covers all aspects of the solution product, including:

- The process by which the solution is arrived at;
- The environment in which it is constructed;
- The design, construction, testing, operation, and functions of the solution product itself.

Confusing the *problem* with the *solution* is one of the great dangers of IT projects, resulting in software that may be a very good solution to *some* problem, but not to the specific set of problems its users face. See the quotation from Gamma *et al.* under Problem domain

Software Product Development Challenges

1. Project Infrastructure Issues

An unestablished project environment is always a common challenge in terms of its impact on project delivery. To ensure efficient project development, test and pre-production environments should be made available during the development, testing, and user acceptance testing (UAT) phases. If the environment is not available, then there is no way you can proceed with your project on time and under budget.

2. Requirements Volatility

A major reason for the complexity of software projects is the constant changing of requirements. Not surprisingly, 33% of the respondents of the 2016 Stack Overflow Developer Survey consider building products with unspecific requirements, as their biggest challenge. Requirements gathering is a lot more than a handful of business consultants coming up with their ideal product – it is understanding fully what a project will deliver.

- Define and agree on the scope of the project
- Don't assume end user needs and requirements – make sure the project team fully understands the needs and it's been communicated in between teams clearly
- While refurbishing a product, involve users from the start, and in the case of new product development, consider UX from the start
- Create a clear, concise and thorough requirements document and confirm your understanding of the requirements
- And if necessary, create a prototype to confirm and/or refine final agreed upon requirements

3. Ignoring Best Code Development Practices

Not reviewing code, or suppressing errors are just a means that developers use to save time and meet deadlines. Following a formal quality assurance process is imperative for a successful launch. If you witness developers trying to cut corners in the development process, discourage it immediately. Encourage them to use best code development practices to meet the requirements sooner and in a more efficient manner.

4. Undefined Quality Standards

Defect identification is inevitable during functionality testing, even if the product has been through thorough unit testing during the development phase. When you come out with the test approach, scenarios, conditions, cases, and scripts to complete the functional testing of your project, make sure your test plan covers all the requirements that are to be delivered by planning several cycles of testing.

5. Adapting the Latest Market Trends

Catering to the latest technology requirements such as mobile first or mobile-only or desktop-first is often challenging. If you don't have resources with hands-on experience in the latest and trending technologies, it is sure to impact your time to market. Make sure your resources constantly polish their skills to remain relevant.

6. Managing Design Influences

Product designs are under constant influence from stakeholders, the development organization, and other developmental factors. Managing these influences is essential for maximizing the quality of systems and their related influence on future business opportunities. The increase of easily accessible, simple applications has resulted in user expectations growing exponentially. Make sure you streamline your design and offer a consistent experience across devices, operating systems, and form factors.

7. The integration Challenge

There are thousands of different technologies, systems, and applications available for businesses. Integrating third-party or other custom applications, such as your ERP, website, or inventory management database adds substantial complexity to your project. And the bigger challenge with integration is that they remain hidden throughout the development process, and surface only at the end, leading to extra costs, delays, lowered quality, and sometimes even failure of the project. If you want your software solution to conform to the external constraints of other systems, you should:

- Get a clear understanding of end-user requirements
- Implement an enterprise-wide framework which works as a platform of structuring the application
- Discover and research new technologies, design and develop new solutions, and then test and evaluate them to ensure optimum integration
- Pay extra attention to research and development, testing, and prototyping.
- Test, test, and test again before deploying the solution

8. Juggling Projects and Tasks

Very often multi-tasking might give you more trouble than expected. Resources cannot focus on a single task or module if their manager bombards them with tasks.

"To be successful in project management you absolutely have to be an excellent planner," says Ryan Chan, founder and CEO of UpKeep Maintenance Management.

And, one obvious way to be an excellent planner is to leverage project management tools like Project Pro in O365 and keep projects, resources, and teams organized and on track. Stay on track, meet all deadlines, work seamlessly across applications, and efficiently and effortlessly manage your projects. Always keep task allocation sequential rather than parallel, and encourage resources to give their best in whatever they do.

9. Test Environment Duplication

Testing a software system in a controlled environment is difficult since the user is not immersed in a completely realistic working situation. It's impractical to gauge how a user will really use the application in different situations on a regular basis until it's deployed. However, with software applications for both B2B and B2C segments becoming more and more diversified than in the past, controlled testing is not sufficient. Therefore, testing the software or app or product in a separate real-life test environment is critical to your software's success.

10. The Security Challenge

Security breaches are on the rise; a recent study estimates that 96% of all web applications contain at least one serious vulnerability. How do you cope with evolving security threats? How do you keep each layer of your software or application secure?

- Look beyond technology to improve security of your software
- Develop your software using high-level programming languages with built-in security features
- Make security assurance activities such as penetration testing, code review, and architecture analysis an integral part of the development effort
- Perform all the essential core activities to produce secure applications and systems including conceptual definition, control specification, design and code review, system test review, and maintenance and change management
- Make sure security is not just the responsibility of the software engineer but also the responsibility of all the stakeholders involved including the management, project managers, business analysts, quality assurance managers, technical architects, and application and developers

System Design Strategy

A good system design is to organise the program modules in such a way that are easy to develop and change. Structured design techniques help developers to deal with the size and complexity of programs. Analysts create instructions for the developers about how code should be written and how pieces of code should fit together to form a program.

Importance :

1. If any pre-existing code needs to be understood, organised and pieced together.
2. It is common for the project team to have to write some code and produce original programs that support the application logic of the system.

There are many strategies or techniques for performing system design. They are:

1. **Bottom-up approach:**
   The design starts with the lowest level components and subsystems. By using these components, the next immediate higher level components and subsystems are created or composed. The process is continued till all the components and subsystems are composed into a single component, which is considered as the complete system. The amount of abstraction grows high as the design moves to more high levels.

By using the basic information existing system, when a new system needs to be created, the bottom up strategy suits the purpose.
   Advantages:

   - The economics can result when general solutions can be reused.
   - It can be used to hide the low-level details of implementation and be merged with top-down technique.

   Disadvantages:

   - It is not so closely related to the structure of the problem.
   - High quality bottom-up solutions are very hard to construct.
   - It leads to proliferation of 'potentially useful' functions rather than most approprite ones.

2. **Top-down approach:**
   Each system is divided into several subsystems and components. Each of the subsystem is further divided into set of subsystems and components. This process of division facilitates in forming a system hierarchy

structure. The complete software system is considered as a single entity and in relation to the characteristics, the system is split into sub-system and component. The same is done with each of the sub-system.

This process is continued until the lowest level of the system is reached. The design is started initially by defining the system as a whole and then keeps on adding definitions of the subsystems and components. When all the definitions are combined together, it turns out to be a complete system.

For the solutions of the software need to be developed from the ground level, top-down design best suits the purpose.

Advantages:

• The main advantage of top down approach is that its strong focus on requirements helps to make a design responsive according to its requirements.

Disadvantages:

• Project and system boundries tends to be application specification oriented. Thus it is more likely that advantages of component reuse will be missed.
• The system is likely to miss, the benefits of a well-structured, simple architecture.

SDLC Cycle

SDLC Cycle represents the process of developing software.

Below is the diagrammatic representation of the SDLC cycle

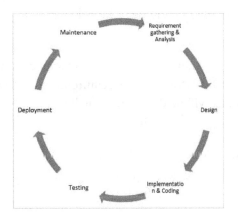

SDLC Phases

Given below are the various phases:

- Requirement gathering and analysis
  - Design
- Implementation or coding
  - Testing
  - Deployment
  - Maintenance

#1) Requirement Gathering and Analysis

During this phase, all the relevant information is collected from the customer to develop a product as per their expectation. Any ambiguities must be resolved in this phase only.

Business analyst and Project Manager set up a meeting with the customer to gather all the information like what the customer wants to build, who will be the end-user, what is the purpose of the product. Before building a product a core understanding or knowledge of the product is very important.

For Example, A customer wants to have an application which involves money transactions. In this case, the requirement has to be clear like what kind of transactions will be done, how it will be done, in which currency it will be done, etc.

Once the requirement gathering is done, an analysis is done to check the feasibility of the development of a product. In case of any ambiguity, a call is set up for further discussion.

Once the requirement is clearly understood, the SRS (Software Requirement Specification) document is created. This document should be thoroughly understood by the developers and also should be reviewed by the customer for future reference.

#2) Design : In this phase, the requirement gathered in the SRS document is used as an input and software architecture that is used for implementing system development is derived.

#3) Implementation or Coding :Implementation/Coding starts once the developer gets the Design document. The Software design is translated into source code. All the components of the software are implemented in this phase.

#4) Testing : *Testing starts once the coding is complete and the modules are released for testing. In this phase, the developed software is tested thoroughly and any defects found are assigned to developers to get them fixed.*

Retesting, regression testing is done until the point at which the software is as per the customer's expectation. Testers refer SRS document to make sure that the software is as per the customer's standard.

#5) Deployment : *Once the product is tested, it is deployed in the production environment or first UAT (User Acceptance testing) is done depending on the customer expectation.*

In the case of UAT, a replica of the production environment is created and the customer along with the developers does the testing. If the customer finds the application as expected, then sign off is provided by the customer to go live.

#6) Maintenance : *After the deployment of a product on the production environment, maintenance of the product i.e. if any issue comes up and needs to be fixed or any enhancement is to be done is taken care by the developers.*

Software Development Life Cycle Models

A software life cycle model is a descriptive representation of the software development cycle. SDLC models might have a different approach but the basic phases and activity remain the same for all the models.

#1) Waterfall Model :*Waterfall model is the very first model that is used in SDLC. It is also known as the linear sequential model.*

In this model, the outcome of one phase is the input for the next phase. Development of the next phase starts only when the previous phase is complete.

- First, Requirement gathering and analysis is done. Once the requirement is freeze then only the System Design can start. Herein, the SRS document created is the output for the Requirement phase and it acts as an input for the System Design.
- In System Design Software architecture and Design, documents which act as an input for the next phase are created i.e. Implementation and coding.
- In the Implementation phase, coding is done and the software developed is the input for the next phase i.e. testing.
- In the testing phase, the developed code is tested thoroughly to detect the defects in the software. Defects are logged into the defect tracking tool and are retested once fixed. Bug logging, Retest, Regression testing goes on until the time the software is in go-live state.
- In the Deployment phase, the developed code is moved into production after the sign off is given by the customer.
- Any issues in the production environment are resolved by the developers which come under maintenance

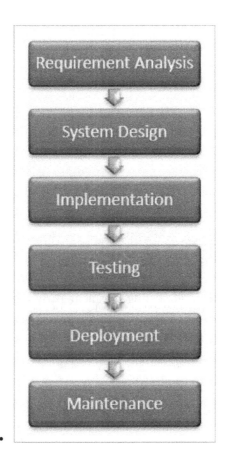

-

Advantages of the Waterfall Model:

- Waterfall model is the simple model which can be easily understood and is the one in which all the phases are done step by step.
- Deliverables of each phase are well defined, and this leads to no complexity and makes the project easily manageable.

Disadvantages of Waterfall model:

- Waterfall model is time-consuming & cannot be used in the short duration projects as in this model a new phase cannot be started until the ongoing phase is completed.
- Waterfall model cannot be used for the projects which have uncertain requirement or wherein the requirement keeps on changing as this model expects the requirement to be clear in the requirement gathering and analysis phase itself and any change in the later stages would lead to cost higher as the changes would be required in all the phases.

#2) V-Shaped Model

V- Model is also known as Verification and Validation Model. In this model Verification & Validation goes hand in hand i.e. development and testing goes parallel. V model and waterfall model are the same except that the test planning and testing start at an early stage in V-Model.

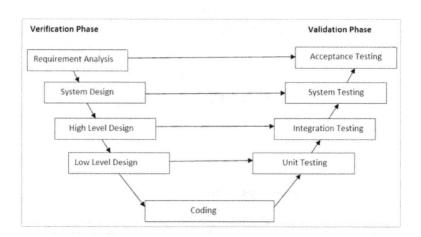

a) Verification Phase:

(i) Requirement Analysis:

In this phase, all the required information is gathered & analyzed. Verification activities include reviewing the requirements.

(ii) System Design:

Once the requirement is clear, a system is designed i.e. architecture, components of the product are created and documented in a design document.

(iii) High-Level Design:

High-level design defines the architecture/design of modules. It defines the functionality between the two modules.

(iv) Low-Level Design:

Low-level Design defines the architecture/design of individual components.

(v) Coding:

Code development is done in this phase.

b) Validation Phase:

(i) Unit Testing:

Unit testing is performed using the unit test cases that are designed and is done in the Low-level design phase. Unit testing is performed by the developer itself. It is performed on individual components which lead to early defect detection.

(ii) Integration Testing:

Integration testing is performed using integration test cases in High-level Design phase. Integration testing is the testing that is done on integrated modules. It is performed by testers.

(iii) System Testing:

System testing is performed in the System Design phase. In this phase, the complete system is tested i.e. the entire system functionality is tested.

(iv) Acceptance Testing:

Acceptance testing is associated with the Requirement Analysis phase and is done in the customer's environment.

Advantages of V – Model:

- It is a simple and easily understandable model.
- V –model approach is good for smaller projects wherein the requirement is defined and it freezes in the early stage.
- It is a systematic and disciplined model which results in a high-quality product.

Disadvantages of V-Model:

- V-shaped model is not good for ongoing projects.
- Requirement change at the later stage would cost too high.

#3) Prototype Model

The prototype model is a model in which the prototype is developed prior to the actual software.

Prototype models have limited functional capabilities and inefficient performance when compared to the actual software. Dummy functions are used to create prototypes. This is a valuable mechanism for understanding the customers' needs.

Software prototypes are built prior to the actual software to get valuable feedback from the customer. Feedbacks are implemented and the prototype is again reviewed by the customer for any change. This process goes on until the model is accepted by the customer.

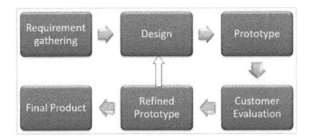

Once the requirement gathering is done, the quick design is created and the prototype which is presented to the customer for evaluation is built.

Customer feedback and the refined requirement is used to modify the prototype and is again presented to the customer for evaluation. Once the customer approves the prototype, it is used as a requirement for building the actual software. The actual software is build using the Waterfall model approach.

Advantages of Prototype model:

- Users are actively involved in the development
- Since in this methodology a working model of the system is provided, the users get a better understanding of the system being developed.
- Errors can be detected much earlier.
- Quicker user feedback is available leading to better solutions.
- Missing functionality can be identified easily
- Confusing or difficult functions can be identified
- Requirements validation, Quick implementation of, incomplete, but functional, application.

Disadvantages of Prototype model:

- Leads to implementing and then repairing way of building systems.

- Practically, this methodology may increase the complexity of the system as scope of the system may expand beyond original plans.
- Incomplete application may cause application not to be used as the
  - full system was designed
- Incomplete or inadequate problem analysis.

Use of Prototype model:

- Prototype model should be used when the desired system needs to have a lot of interaction with the end users.
- Typically, online systems, web interfaces have a very high amount of interaction with end users, are best suited for Prototype model. It might take a while for a system to be built that allows ease of use and needs minimal training for the end user.
- Prototyping ensures that the end users constantly work with the system and provide a feedback which is incorporated in the prototype to result in a useable system. They are excellent for designing good human computer interface systems.

#4) Spiral Model :The Spiral Model includes iterative and prototype approach. Spiral model phases are followed in the iterations. The loops in the model represent the phase of the SDLC process i.e. the innermost loop is of requirement gathering & analysis which follows the Planning, Risk analysis, development, and evaluation. Next loop is Designing followed by Implementation & then testing.

Spiral Model has four phases:

- Planning
- Risk Analysis
- Engineering
- Evaluation

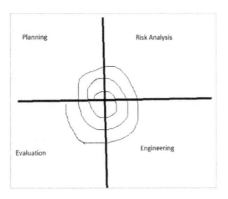

(i) Planning:

The planning phase includes requirement gathering wherein all the required information is gathered from the customer and is documented. Software requirement specification document is created for the next phase.

(ii) Risk Analysis:

In this phase, the best solution is selected for the risks involved and analysis is done by building the prototype.

For Example, the risk involved in accessing the data from a remote database can be that the data access rate might be too slow. The risk can be resolved by building a prototype of the data access subsystem.

(iii) Engineering:

Once the risk analysis is done, coding and testing are done.

(iv) Evaluation:

Customer evaluates the developed system and plans for the next iteration.

Advantages of Spiral Model:

- Risk Analysis is done extensively using the prototype models.
- Any enhancement or change in the functionality can be done in the next iteration.

Disadvantages of Spiral Model:

- The spiral model is best suited for large projects only.
- The cost can be high as it might take a large number of iterations which can lead to high time to reach the final product.

#5) Iterative Incremental Model

The iterative incremental model divides the product into small chunks.

For Example, Feature to be developed in the iteration is decided and implemented. Each iteration goes through the phases namely Requirement Analysis, Designing, Coding, and Testing. Detailed planning is not required in iterations.

Once the iteration is completed, a product is verified and is delivered to the customer for their evaluation and feedback. Customer's feedback is implemented in the next iteration along with the newly added feature.

Hence, the product increments in terms of features and once the iterations are completed the final build holds all the features of the product.

Phases of Iterative & Incremental Development Model:

- Inception phase
- Elaboration Phase
- Construction Phase
- Transition Phase

(i) Inception Phase:

Inception phase includes the requirement and scope of the Project.

(ii) Elaboration Phase:

In the elaboration phase, the working architecture of a product is delivered which covers the risk identified in the inception phase and also fulfills the non-functional requirements.

(iii) Construction Phase:

In the Construction phase, the architecture is filled in with the code which is ready to be deployed and is created through analysis, designing, implementation, and testing of the functional requirement.

(iv) Transition Phase:

In the Transition Phase, the product is deployed in the Production environment.

Advantages of Iterative & Incremental Model:

- Any change in the requirement can be easily done and would not cost as there is a scope of incorporating the new requirement in the next iteration.
- Risk is analyzed & identified in the iterations.
- Defects are detected at an early stage.
- As the product is divided into smaller chunks it is easy to manage the product.

Disadvantages of Iterative & Incremental Model:

- Complete requirement and understanding of a product are required to break down and build incrementally.

#6) Big Bang Model

Big Bang Model does not have any defined process. Money and efforts are put together as the input and output come as a developed product which might be or might not be the same as what the customer needs.

Big Bang Model does not require much planning and scheduling. The developer does the requirement analysis & coding and develops the product as per his understanding. This model is used for small projects only. There is no testing team and no formal testing is done, and this could be a cause for the failure of the project.

Advantages of Big Bang Model:

- It's a very simple Model.
- Less Planning and scheduling is required.
- The developer has the flexibility to build the software of their own.

Disadvantages of the Big Bang Model:

- Big Bang models cannot be used for large, ongoing & complex projects.
- High risk and uncertainty.

#7) Agile Model

Agile Model is a combination of the Iterative and incremental model. This model focuses more on flexibility while developing a product rather than on the requirement.

In Agile, a product is broken into small incremental builds. It is not developed as a complete product in one go. Each build increments in terms of features. The next build is built on previous functionality.

In agile iterations are termed as sprints. Each sprint lasts for2-4 weeks. At the end of each sprint, the product owner verifies the product and after his approval, it is delivered to the customer.

Customer feedback is taken for improvement and his suggestions and enhancement are worked on in the next sprint. Testing is done in each sprint to minimize the risk of any failures.

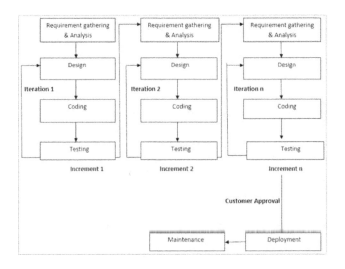

Advantages of Agile Model:

- It allows more flexibility to adapt to the changes.
- The new feature can be added easily.
- Customer satisfaction as the feedback and suggestions are taken at every stage.

Disadvantages:

- Lack of documentation.
- Agile needs experienced and highly skilled resources.
- If a customer is not clear about how exactly they want the product to be, then the project would fail.

Conclusion

Adherence to a suitable life cycle is very important, for the successful completion of the Project. This, in turn, makes the management easier.

Different Software Development Life Cycle models have their own Pros and Cons. The best model for any Project can be determined by the factors like Requirement (whether it is clear or unclear), System Complexity, Size of the Project, Cost, Skill limitation, etc.

Example, in case of an unclear requirement, Spiral and Agile models are best to be used as the required change can be accommodated easily at any stage.Waterfall model is a basic model and all the other SDLC models are based on that only.

Common Advantages and disadvantages of Models

Model	advantages	disadvantages
Waterfall Model	1. Easy to understand and implement 2. Reinforces good habits: define-before-design and design-before-code. 3. Identifies deliverables and milestones 4. Works well on mature deliverables	1. Real projects rarely follow sequential approach 2. Uncertainty at the beginning of the development 3. No working version of the system until very late
Incremental Model	1. Divides project into smaller parts 2. Creates working model early 3. Feedback from one phase provides information for the next phase 4. Very useful when more staffing is unavailable	1. Users need to be actively involved in the project. 2. Communication and coordination skills are central process 3. Informal requests for improvement for each phase may lead to confusion 4. It may lead to scope creep
Spiral Model	1. Designed to include the best features form Waterfall and Prototyping Model 2. Good for large and mission-critical projects 3. Introduces risk assessment as a new component	1. Can be a costly model to use 2. Risk analysis requires specific expertise 3. Project's success is highly dependent on risk analysis phase 4. Doesn't work well for smaller projects

Software Characteristics

Software is defined as collection of computer programs, procedures, rules and data. Software Characteristics are classified into six major components:

These components are described below:

- **Functionality:**
It refers to the degree of performance of the software against its intended purpose.

- **Reliability:**
A set of attribute that bear on capability of software to maintain its level of performance under the given condition for a stated period of time.

- **Efficiency:**
It refers to the ability of the software to use system resources in the most effective and efficient manner.the software should make effective use of storage space and executive command as per desired timing requirement.

- **Usability:**
It refers to the extent to which the software can be used with ease.the amount of effort or time required to learn how to use the software.

- **Maintainability:**
It refers to the ease with which the modifications can be made in a software system to extend its functionality, improve its performance, or correct errors.

- **Portability:**
A set of attribute that bear on the ability of software to be transferred from one environment to another, without or minimum changes.

CHAPTER TWO

PROJECT MANAGEMENT PROCESS

Project Management is the application of knowledge, skills, tools and techniques to project activities to meet the project requirements.

Project Management Process consists of the following 4 stages:

- Feasibility study
- Project Planning
- Project Execution
- Project Termination

Feasibility Study:

Feasibility study explores system requirements to determine project feasibility. There are several fields of feasibility study including economic feasibility, operational feasibility, technical feasibility. The goal is to determine whether the system can be implemented or not. The process of feasibility study takes as input the requirement details as specified by the user and other domain-specific details. The output of this process simply tells whether the project should be undertaken or not and if yes, what would the constraints be. Additionally, all the risks and their potential effects on the projects are also evaluated before a decision to start the project is taken.

Project Planning:

A detailed plan stating stepwise strategy to achieve the listed objectives is an integral part of any project.

Planning consists of the following activities:

- Set objectives or goals
- Develop strategies
- Develop project policies
- Determine courses of action
- Making planning decisions
- Set procedures and rules for the project
- Develop a software project plan
- Prepare budget
- Conduct risk management
- Document software project plans

This step also involves the construction of a work breakdown structure(WBS). It also includes size, effort, schedule and cost estimation using various techniques.

Project Execution:
A project is executed by choosing an appropriate software development lifecycle model(SDLC). It includes a number of steps including requirements analysis, design, coding, testing and implementation, testing, delivery and maintenance. There are a number of factors that need to be considered while doing so including the size of the system, the nature of the project, time and budget constraints, domain requirements, etc. An inappropriate SDLC can lead to failure of the project.

Project Termination:
There can be several reasons for the termination of a project. Though expecting a project to terminate after successful completion is conventional, but at times, a project may also terminate without completion. Projects have to be closed down when the requirements are not fulfilled according to given time and cost constraints.
Some of the reasons for failure include:

- Fast changing technology
- Project running out of time
- Organizational politics
- Too much change in customer requirements
- Project exceeding budget or funds

Once the project is terminated, a post-performance analysis is done. Also, a final report is published describing the experiences, lessons learned, recommendations for handling future projects.

=====================================

The job pattern of an IT company engaged in software development can be seen split in two parts:

1. Software Creation
2. Software Project Managemen

A project is well-defined task, which is a collection of several operations done in order to achieve a goal (for example, software development and delivery). A Project can be characterized as:

- Every project may has a unique and distinct goal.
- Project is not routine activity or day-to-day operations.
- Project comes with a start time and end time.
- Project ends when its goal is achieved hence it is a temporary phase in the lifetime of an organization.
- Project needs adequate resources in terms of time, manpower, finance, material and knowledge-bank.

Software Project

A Software Project is the complete procedure of software development from requirement gathering to testing and maintenance, carried out according to the execution methodologies, in a specified period of time to achieve intended software product.

Need of software project management

Software is said to be an intangible product. Software development is a kind of all new stream in world business and there's very little experience in building software products. Most software products are tailor made to fit client's requirements. The most important is that the underlying technology changes and advances so frequently and rapidly that experience of one product may not be applied to the other one. All such business and environmental constraints bring risk in software development hence it is essential to manage software projects efficiently.

The image above shows triple constraints for software projects. It is an essential part of software organization to deliver quality product, keeping the cost within client's budget constrain and deliver the project as per scheduled. There are several factors, both internal and external, which may impact this triple constrain triangle. Any of three factor can severely impact the other two.

Therefore, software project management is essential to incorporate user requirements along with budget and time constraints.

Software Project Manager

A software project manager is a person who undertakes the responsibility of executing the software project. Software project manager is thoroughly aware of all the phases of SDLC that the software would go through. Project manager may never directly involve in producing the end product but he controls and manages the activities involved in production.

A project manager closely monitors the development process, prepares and executes various plans, arranges necessary and adequate resources, maintains communication among all team members in order to address issues of cost, budget, resources, time, quality and customer satisfaction.

Let us see few responsibilities that a project manager shoulders -

- Managing People
- Act as project leader
- Liaison with stakeholders
- Managing human resources
- Setting up reporting hierarchy etc.
- Managing Project
- Defining and setting up project scope
- Managing project management activities
- Monitoring progress and performance
- Risk analysis at every phase
- Take necessary step to avoid or come out of problems
- Act as project spokesperson

Software Management Activities

Software project management comprises of a number of activities, which contains planning of project, deciding scope of software product, estimation of cost in various terms, scheduling of tasks and events, and resource management. Project management activities may include:

Project Planning
Scope Management
Project Estimation
Project Planning

Software project planning is task, which is performed before the production of software actually starts. It is there for the software production but involves no concrete activity that has any direction connection with software production; rather it is a set of multiple processes, which facilitates software production. Project planning may include the following:

Scope Management

It defines the scope of project; this includes all the activities, process need to be done in order to make a deliverable software product. Scope management is essential because it creates boundaries of the project by clearly defining what would be done in the project and what would not be done. This makes project to contain limited and quantifiable tasks, which can easily be documented and in turn avoids cost and time overrun.

During Project Scope management, it is necessary to -

* Define the scope
* Decide its verification and control
* Divide the project into various smaller parts for ease of management.
* Verify the scope
* Control the scope by incorporating changes to the scope

Project Estimation

For an effective management accurate estimation of various measures is a must. With correct estimation managers can manage and control the project more efficiently and effectively.

Project estimation may involve the following:

Software size estimation

Software size may be estimated either in terms of KLOC (Kilo Line of Code) or by calculating number of function points in the software. Lines of code depend upon coding practices and Function points vary according to the user or software requirement.

Effort estimation

The managers estimate efforts in terms of personnel requirement and man-hour required to produce the software. For effort estimation software size should be known. This can either be derived by managers' experience, organization's historical data or software size can be converted into efforts by using some standard formulae.

Time estimation

Once size and efforts are estimated, the time required to produce the software can be estimated. Efforts required is segregated into sub categories as per the requirement specifications and interdependency of various components of software. Software tasks are divided into smaller tasks, activities or events by Work Breakthrough Structure (WBS). The tasks are scheduled on day-to-day basis or in calendar months.

The sum of time required to complete all tasks in hours or days is the total time invested to complete the project.

Cost estimation

This might be considered as the most difficult of all because it depends on more elements than any of the previous ones. For estimating project cost, it is required to consider -

- Size of software
- Software quality
- Hardware
- Additional software or tools, licenses etc.
- Skilled personnel with task-specific skills
- Travel involved
- Communication
- Training and support
- Project Estimation Techniques
-

Project manager can estimate the listed factors using two broadly recognized techniques –

Decomposition Technique

This technique assumes the software as a product of various compositions.

There are two main models -

Line of Code Estimation is done on behalf of number of line of codes in the software product.

Function Points Estimation is done on behalf of number of function points in the software product.

Empirical Estimation Technique

This technique uses empirically derived formulae to make estimation. These formulae are based on LOC or FPs.

Putnam Model

This model is made by Lawrence H. Putnam, which is based on Norden's frequency distribution (Rayleigh curve). Putnam model maps time and efforts required with software size.

COCOMO

COCOMO stands for COnstructive COst MOdel, developed by Barry W. Boehm. It divides the software product into three categories of software: organic, semi-detached and embedded.

Project Scheduling

Project Scheduling in a project refers to roadmap of all activities to be done with specified order and within time slot allotted to each activity. Project managers tend to define various tasks, and project milestones and arrange them keeping various factors in mind. They look for tasks lie in critical path in the schedule, which are necessary to complete in specific manner (because of task interdependency) and strictly within the time allocated. Arrangement of tasks which lies out of critical path are less likely to impact over all schedule of the project.

For scheduling a project, it is necessary to -

- Break down the project tasks into smaller, manageable form
- Find out various tasks and correlate them
- Estimate time frame required for each task
- Divide time into work-units
- Assign adequate number of work-units for each task
- Calculate total time required for the project from start to finish

Resource management

All elements used to develop a software product may be assumed as resource for that project. This may include human resource, productive tools and software libraries.

The resources are available in limited quantity and stay in the organization as a pool of assets. The shortage of resources hampers the development of project and it can lag behind the schedule. Allocating extra resources increases development cost in the end. It is therefore necessary to estimate and allocate adequate resources for the project.

Resource management includes-

- Defining proper organization project by creating a project team and allocating responsibilities to each team member
- Determining resources required at a particular stage and their availability
- Manage Resources by generating resource request when they are required and de-allocating them when they are no more needed.

Project Risk Management

Risk management involves all activities pertaining to identification, analyzing and making provision for predictable and non-predictable risks in the project. Risk may include the following:

- Experienced staff leaving the project and new staff coming in.
- Change in organizational management.
- Requirement change or misinterpreting requirement.
- Under-estimation of required time and resources.
- Technological changes, environmental changes, business competition.

Risk Management Process

There are following activities involved in risk management process:

Identification- Make note of all possible risks, which may occur in the project.

Categorize - Categorize known risks into high, medium and low risk intensity as per their possible impact on the project.

Manage - Analyze the probability of occurrence of risks at various phases. Make plan to avoid or face risks. Attempt to minimize their side-effects.

Monitor - Closely monitor the potential risks and their early symptoms. Also monitor the effects of steps taken to mitigate or avoid them.

Project Execution & Monitoring

In this phase, the tasks described in project plans are executed according to their schedules.

Execution needs monitoring in order to check whether everything is going according to the plan. Monitoring is observing to check the probability of risk and taking measures to address the risk or report the status of various tasks.

These measures include -

Activity Monitoring- All activities scheduled within some task can be monitored on day-to-day basis. When all activities in a task are completed, it is considered as complete.

Status Reports - The reports contain status of activities and tasks completed within a given time frame, generally a week. Status can be marked as finished, pending or work-in-progress etc.

Milestones Checklist - Every project is divided into multiple phases where major tasks are performed (milestones) based on the phases of SDLC. This milestone checklist is prepared once every few weeks and reports the status of milestones.

Project Communication Management

Effective communication plays vital role in the success of a project. It bridges gaps between client and the organization, among the team members as well as other stake holders in the project such as hardware suppliers.

Communication can be oral or written. Communication management process may have the following steps:

Planning - This step includes the identifications of all the stakeholders in the project and the mode of communication among them. It also considers if any additional communication facilities are required.

Sharing - After determining various aspects of planning, manager focuses on sharing correct information with the correct person on correct time. This keeps every one involved the project up to date with project progress and its status.

Feedback -Project managers use various measures and feedback mechanism and create status and performance reports. This mechanism ensures that input from various stakeholders is coming to the project manager as their feedback.

Closure - At the end of each major event, end of a phase of SDLC or end of the project itself, administrative closure is formally announced to update every stakeholder by sending email, by distributing a hardcopy of document or by other mean of effective communication.

After closure, the team moves to next phase or project.

Configuration Management

Configuration management is a process of tracking and controlling the changes in software in terms of the requirements, design, functions and development of the product.

IEEE defines it as "the process of identifying and defining the items in the system, controlling the change of these items throughout their life cycle, recording and reporting the status of items and change requests, and verifying the completeness and correctness of items".

Generally, once the SRS is finalized there is less chance of requirement of changes from user. If they occur, the changes are addressed only with prior approval of higher management, as there is a possibility of cost and time overrun.

Baseline

A phase of SDLC is assumed over if it baselined, i.e. baseline is a measurement that defines completeness of a phase. A phase is baselined when all activities pertaining to it are finished and well documented. If it was not the final phase, its output would be used in next immediate phase.

Configuration management is a discipline of organization administration, which takes care of occurrence of any change (process, requirement, technological, strategical etc.) after a phase is baselined. CM keeps check on any changes done in software.

Change Control

Change control is function of configuration management, which ensures that all changes made to software system are consistent and made as per organizational rules and regulations.

A change in the configuration of product goes through following steps -

Identification - A change request arrives from either internal or external source. When change request is identified formally, it is properly documented.

Validation -Validity of the change request is checked and its handling procedure is confirmed.

Analysis - The impact of change request is analyzed in terms of schedule, cost and required efforts. Overall impact of the prospective change on system is analyzed.

Control -If the prospective change either impacts too many entities in the system or it is unavoidable, it is mandatory to take approval of high authorities before change is incorporated into the system. It is decided if the change is worth incorporation or not. If it is not, change request is refused formally.

Execution - If the previous phase determines to execute the change request, this phase take appropriate actions to execute the change, does a thorough revision if necessary.

Close request -The change is verified for correct implementation and merging with the rest of the system. This newly incorporated change in the software is documented properly and the request is formally is closed.

Project Management Tools

The risk and uncertainty rises multifold with respect to the size of the project, even when the project is developed according to set methodologies.

There are tools available, which aid for effective project management. A few are described -

Gantt Chart

Gantt charts was devised by Henry Gantt (1917). It represents project schedule with respect to time periods. It is a horizontal bar chart with bars representing activities and time scheduled for the project activities.

PERT Chart

PERT (Program Evaluation & Review Technique) chart is a tool that depicts project as network diagram. It is capable of graphically representing main events of project in both parallel and consecutive way. Events, which occur one after another, show dependency of the later event over the previous one.

Events are shown as numbered nodes. They are connected by labeled arrows depicting sequence of tasks in the project.

Resource Histogram

This is a graphical tool that contains bar or chart representing number of resources (usually skilled staff) required over time for a project event (or phase). Resource Histogram is an effective tool for staff planning and coordination.

Critical Path Analysis

This tools is useful in recognizing interdependent tasks in the project. It also helps to find out the shortest path or critical path to complete the project successfully. Like PERT diagram, each event is allotted a specific time frame. This tool shows dependency of event assuming an event can proceed to next only if the previous one is completed.

The events are arranged according to their earliest possible start time. Path between start and end node is critical path which cannot be further reduced and all events require to be executed in same order.

COCOMO Model

Cocomo (Constructive Cost Model) is a regression model based on LOC, i.e **number of Lines of Code**. It is a procedural cost estimate model for software projects and often used as a process of reliably predicting the various parameters associated with making a project such as size, effort, cost, time and quality. It was proposed by Barry Boehm in 1970 and is based on the study of 63 projects, which make it one of the best-documented models.

The key parameters which define the quality of any software products, which are also an outcome of the Cocomo are primarily Effort & Schedule:

- **Effort:** Amount of labor that will be required to complete a task. It is measured in person-months units.
- **Schedule:** Simply means the amount of time required for the completion of the job, which is, of course, proportional to the effort put. It is measured in the units of time such as weeks, months.

Different models of Cocomo have been proposed to predict the cost estimation at different levels, based on the amount of accuracy and correctness required. All of these models can be applied to a variety of projects, whose characteristics determine the value of constant to be used in subsequent calculations. These characteristics pertaining to different system types are mentioned below.

Boehm's definition of organic, semidetached, and embedded systems:

1. **Organic** – A software project is said to be an organic type if the team size required is adequately small, the problem is well understood and has been solved in the past and also the team members have a nominal experience regarding the problem.
2. **Semi-detached** – A software project is said to be a Semi-detached type if the vital characteristics such as team-size, experience, knowledge of

the various programming environment lie in between that of organic and Embedded. The projects classified as Semi-Detached are comparatively less familiar and difficult to develop compared to the organic ones and require more experience and better guidance and creativity. Eg: Compilers or different Embedded Systems can be considered of Semi-Detached type.

3. **Embedded** – A software project with requiring the highest level of complexity, creativity, and experience requirement fall under this category. Such software requires a larger team size than the other two models and also the developers need to be sufficiently experienced and creative to develop such complex models.

All the above system types utilize different values of the constants used in Effort Calculations.

Types of Models: COCOMO consists of a hierarchy of three increasingly detailed and accurate forms. Any of the three forms can be adopted according to our requirements. These are types of COCOMO model:

1. Basic COCOMO Model
2. Intermediate COCOMO Model
3. Detailed COCOMO Model

The first level, **Basic COCOMO** can be used for quick and slightly rough calculations of Software Costs. Its accuracy is somewhat restricted due to the absence of sufficient factor considerations.

Intermediate COCOMO takes these Cost Drivers into account and **Detailed COCOMO** additionally accounts for the influence of individual project phases, i.e in case of Detailed it accounts for both these cost drivers and also calculations are performed phase wise henceforth producing a more accurate result. These two models are further discussed below.

Estimation of Effort: Calculations –

4. Basic Model –

The above formula is used for the cost estimation of for the basic COCOMO model, and also is used in the subsequent models. The constant values a and b for the Basic Model for the different categories of system:

SOFTWARE PROJECTS	A	B
Organic	2.4	1.05
Semi Detached	3.0	1.12
Embedded	3.6	1.20

The effort is measured in Person-Months and as evident from the formula is dependent on Kilo-Lines of code. These formulas are used as such in the Basic Model calculations, as not much consideration of different factors such as reliability, expertise is taken into account, henceforth the estimate is rough.

1. Intermediate Model –

The basic Cocomo model assumes that the effort is only a function of the number of lines of code and some constants evaluated according to the different software system. However, in reality, no system's effort and schedule can be solely calculated on the basis of Lines of Code. For that, various other factors such as reliability, experience, Capability. These factors are known as Cost Drivers and the Intermediate Model utilizes 15 such drivers for cost estimation.

Classification of Cost Drivers and their attributes:

(i) Product attributes –

- Required software reliability extent
- Size of the application database
- The complexity of the product

(ii) Hardware attributes –

- Run-time performance constraints
- Memory constraints
- The volatility of the virtual machine environment
- Required turnabout time

(iii) Personnel attributes –

- Analyst capability
- Software engineering capability
- Applications experience
- Virtual machine experience
- Programming language experience

(iv) Project attributes –

- Use of software tools
- Application of software engineering methods
- Required development schedule

COST DRIVERS	VERY LOW	LOW	NOMINAL	HIGH	VERY HIGH
Product Attributes					
Required Software Reliability	0.75	0.88	1.00	1.15	1.40
Size of Application Database		0.94	1.00	1.08	1.16
Complexity of The Product	0.70	0.85	1.00	1.15	1.30
Hardware Attributes					
Runtime Performance Constraints			1.00	1.11	1.30
Memory Constraints			1.00	1.06	1.21
Volatility of the virtual machine environment		0.87	1.00	1.15	1.30
Required turnabout time		0.94	1.00	1.07	1.15
Personnel attributes					
Analyst capability	1.46	1.19	1.00	0.86	0.71
Applications experience	1.29	1.13	1.00	0.91	0.82
Software engineer capability	1.42	1.17	1.00	0.86	0.70
Virtual machine experience	1.21	1.10	1.00	0.90	
Programming language experience	1.14	1.07	1.00	0.95	
Project Attributes					
Application of software engineering methods	1.24	1.10	1.00	0.91	0.82
Use of software tools	1.24	1.10	1.00	0.91	0.83
Required development schedule	1.23	1.08	1.00	1.04	1.10

The project manager is to rate these 15 different parameters for a particular project on a scale of one to three. Then, depending on these ratings, appropriate cost driver values are taken from the above table. These 15 values are then multiplied to calculate the EAF (Effort Adjustment Factor). The Intermediate COCOMO formula now takes the form:

SOFTWARE PROJECTS	A	B
Organic	3.2	1.05
Semi Detached	3.0	1.12
Embedded	2.8	1.20

1. Detailed Model –

Detailed COCOMO incorporates all characteristics of the intermediate version with an assessment of the cost driver's impact on each step of the software engineering process. The detailed model uses different effort multipliers for each cost driver attribute. In detailed cocomo, the whole software is divided into different modules and then we apply COCOMO in different modules to estimate effort and then sum the effort.

The Six phases of detailed COCOMO are:

1. Planning and requirements
2. System design
3. Detailed design
4. Module code and test

5. Integration and test
6. Cost Constructive model

The effort is calculated as a function of program size and a set of cost drivers are given according to each phase of the software lifecycle.

CHAPTER THREE

SOFTWARE METRICS

A software metric is a measure of software characteristics which are quantifiable or countable. Software metrics are important for many reasons, including measuring software performance, planning work items, measuring productivity, and many other uses.

Within the software development process, there are many metrics that are all related to each other. Software metrics are related to the four functions of management: Planning, Organization, Control, or Improvement.

In this article, we are going to discuss several topics including many examples of software metrics:

- Benefits of Software Metrics
- How Software Metrics Lack Clarity
- How to Track Software Metrics
- Examples of Software Metrics

Benefits of Software Metrics

The goal of tracking and analyzing software metrics is to determine the quality of the current product or process, improve that quality and predict the quality once the software development project is complete. On a more granular level, software development managers are trying to:

- Increase return on investment (ROI)
- Identify areas of improvement
- Manage workloads

- Reduce overtime
- Reduce costs

These goals can be achieved by providing information and clarity throughout the organization about complex software development projects. Metrics are an important component of quality assurance, management, debugging, performance, and estimating costs, and they're valuable for both developers and development team leaders:

- Managers can use software metrics to identify, prioritize, track and communicate any issues to foster better team productivity. This enables effective management and allows assessment and prioritization of problems within software development projects. The sooner managers can detect software problems, the easier and less-expensive the troubleshooting process.
- Software development teams can use software metrics to communicate the status of software development projects, pinpoint and address issues, and monitor, improve on, and better manage their workflow.

Software metrics offer an assessment of the impact of decisions made during software development projects. This helps managers assess and prioritize objectives and performance goals.

How Software Metrics Lack Clarity

Terms used to describe software metrics often have multiple definitions and ways to count or measure characteristics. For example, lines of code (LOC) is a common measure of software development. But there are two ways to count each line of code:

- One is to count each physical line that ends with a return. But some software developers don't accept this count because it may include lines of "dead code" or comments.
- To get around those shortfalls and others, each logical statement could be considered a line of code.

Thus, a single software package could have two very different LOC counts depending on which counting method is used. That makes it difficult to compare software simply by lines of code or any other metric without a standard definition, which is why **establishing a measurement method and consistent units of measurement** to be used throughout the life of the project is crucial.

There is also an issue with how software metrics are used. If an organization uses productivity metrics that emphasize volume of code and errors, software developers could avoid tackling tricky problems to keep their LOC up and error counts down. Software developers who write a large amount of simple code may have great productivity numbers but not great software development skills. Additionally, software metrics shouldn't be monitored simply because they're easy to obtain and display – only metrics that add value to the project and process should be tracked.

How to Track Software Metrics

Software metrics are great for management teams because they offer a quick way to track software development, set goals and measure performance. But oversimplifying software development can distract software developers from goals such as delivering useful software and increasing customer satisfaction.

Of course, none of this matters if the measurements that are used in software metrics are not collected or the data is not analyzed. The first problem is that software development teams may consider it **more important to actually do the work than to measure it**.

It becomes imperative to **make measurement easy to collect or it will not be done**. Make the software metrics work for the software development team so that it can work better. Measuring and analyzing doesn't have to be burdensome or something that gets in the way of creating code. Software metrics should have several important characteristics. They should be:

- Simple and computable
- Consistent and unambiguous (objective)
- Use consistent units of measurement
- Independent of programming languages
- Easy to calibrate and adaptable
- Easy and cost-effective to obtain
- Able to be validated for accuracy and reliability
- Relevant to the development of high-quality software products

This is why software development platforms that automatically measure and track metrics are important. But software development teams and management run the risk of having too much data and not enough emphasis on the software metrics that help deliver useful software to customers.

The technical question of how software metrics are collected, calculated and reported are not as important as deciding how to use software metrics. Patrick Kua outlines four guidelines for an appropriate use of software metrics:

1. Link software metrics to goals.

Often sets of software metrics are communicated to software development teams as goals. So the focus becomes:

- Reducing the lines of codes
- Reducing the number of bugs reported
- Increasing the number of software iterations
- Speeding up the completion of tasks

Focusing on those metrics as targets help software developers reach more important goals such as improving software usefulness and user experience.

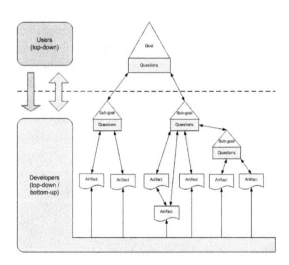

For example, size-based software metrics often measure lines of code to indicate coding complexity or software efficiency. In an effort to reduce the code's complexity, management may place restrictions on how many lines of code are to written to complete functions. In an effort to simplify functions, software developers could write more functions that have fewer lines of code to reach their target but do not reduce overall code complexity or improve software efficiency.

When developing goals, management needs to involve the software development teams in establishing goals, choosing software metrics that measure progress toward those goals and align metrics with those goals.

2. Track trends, not numbers.

Software metrics are very seductive to management because complex processes are represented as simple numbers. And those numbers are easy to compare to other numbers. So when a software metric target is met, it is easy to declare success. Not reaching that number lets software development teams know they need to work more on reaching that target.

These simple targets do not offer as much information on how the software metrics are trending. Any single data point is not as significant as the trend it is part of. Analysis of why the trend line is moving in a certain direction or at what rate it is moving will say more about the process. Trends also will show what effect any process changes have on progress.

The psychological effects of observing a trend – similar to the Hawthorne Effect, or changes in behavior resulting from awareness of being observed – can be greater than focusing on a single measurement. If the target is not met, that, unfortunately, can be seen as a failure. But a trend line showing progress toward a target offers incentive and insight into how to reach that target.

3. Set shorter measurement periods.

Software development teams want to spend their time getting the work done not checking if they are reaching management established targets. So a hands-off approach might be to set the target sometime in the future and not bother the software team until it is time to tell them they succeeded or failed to reach the target.

By breaking the measurement periods into smaller time frames, the software development team can check the software metrics — and the trend line — to determine how well they are progressing.

Yes, that is an interruption, but giving software development teams more time to analyze their progress and change tactics when something is not working is very productive. The shorter periods of measurement offer more data points that can be useful in reaching goals, not just software metric targets.

4. Stop using software metrics that do not lead to change.

We all know that the process of repeating actions without change with the expectation of different results is the definition of insanity. But repeating the same work without adjustments that do not achieve goals is the definition of managing by metrics.

Why would software developers keep doing something that is not getting them closer to goals such as better software experiences? Because they are focusing on software metrics that do not measure progress toward that goal.

Some software metrics have no value when it comes to indicating software quality or team workflow. Management and software development teams need to work on software metrics that drive progress towards goals and provide verifiable, consistent indicators of progress.

Examples of Software Metrics

There is no standard or definition of software metrics that have value to software development teams. And software metrics have different value to different teams. It depends on what are the goals for the software development teams.

As a starting point, here are some software metrics that can help developers track their progress.

Agile process metrics

Agile process metrics focus on how agile teams make decisions and plan. These metrics do not describe the software, but they can be used to improve the software development process.

Lead time

Lead time quantifies how long it takes for ideas to be developed and delivered as software. Lowering lead time is a way to improve how responsive software developers are to customers.

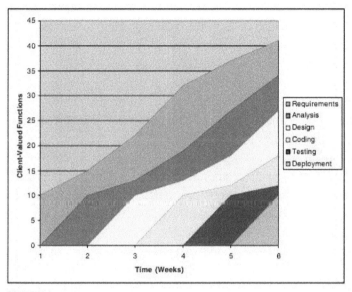

Figure 5-2
Cumulative flow of system inventory.

Cycle time

Cycle time describes how long it takes to change the software system and implement that change in production.

Team velocity

Team velocity measures how many software units a team completes in an iteration or sprint. This is an internal metric that should not be used to compare software development teams. The definition of deliverables changes for individual software development teams over time and the definitions are different for different teams.

Open/close rates

Open/close rates are calculated by tracking production issues reported in a specific time period. It is important to pay attention to how this software metric trends.

Production

Production metrics attempt to measure how much work is done and determine the efficiency of software development teams. The software metrics that use speed as a factor are important to managers who want software delivered as fast as possible.

Active days

Active days is a measure of how much time a software developer contributes code to the software development project. This does not include planning and administrative tasks. The purpose of this software metric is to assess the hidden costs of interruptions.

Assignment scope

Assignment scope is the amount of code that a programmer can maintain and support in a year. This software metric can be used to plan how many people are needed to support a software system and compare teams.

Efficiency

Efficiency attempts to measure the amount of productive code contributed by a software developer. The amount of churn shows the lack of productive code. Thus a software developer with a low churn could have highly efficient code.

Code churn

Code churn represents the number of lines of code that were modified, added or deleted in a specified period of time. If code churn increases, then it could be a sign that the software development project needs attention.

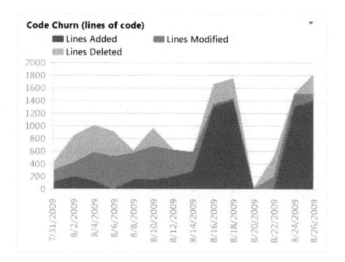

Example Code Churn report, screenshot via Visual Studio

Impact

Impact measures the effect of any code change on the software development project. A code change that affects multiple files could have more impact than a code change affecting a single file.

Mean time between failures (MTBF) and mean time to recover/repair (MTTR)

Both metrics measure how the software performs in the production environment. Since software failures are almost unavoidable, these software metrics attempt to quantify how well the software recovers and preserves data.

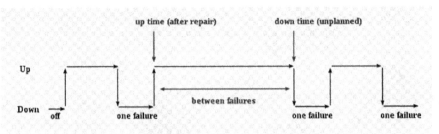

Time Between Failures = { down time - up time}

Application crash rate (ACR)

Application crash rate is calculated by dividing how many times an application fails (F) by how many times it is used (U).

ACR = F/U

Security metrics

Security metrics reflect a measure of software quality. These metrics need to be tracked over time to show how software development teams are developing security responses.

Endpoint incidents

Endpoint incidents are how many devices have been infected by a virus in a given period of time.

Mean time to repair (MTTR)

Mean time to repair in this context measures the time from the security breach discovery to when a working remedy is deployed.

Size-oriented metrics

Size-oriented metrics focus on the size of the software and are usually expressed as kilo lines of code (KLOC). It is a fairly easy software metric to collect once decisions are made about what constitutes a line of code. Unfortunately, it is not useful for comparing software projects written in different languages. Some examples include:

- Errors per KLOC
- Defects per KLOC
- Cost per KLOC

Function-oriented metrics

Function-oriented metrics focus on how much functionality software offers. But functionality cannot be measured directly. So function-oriented software metrics rely on calculating the function point (FP) — a unit of measurement that quantifies the business functionality provided by the product. Function points are also useful for comparing software projects written in different languages.

Function points are not an easy concept to master and methods vary. This is why many software development managers and teams skip function points altogether. They do not perceive function points as worth the time.

Errors per FP or Defects per FP

These software metrics are used as indicators of an information system's quality. Software development teams can use these software metrics to reduce miscommunications and introduce new control measures.

Defect Removal Efficiency (DRE)

The Defect Removal Efficiency is used to quantify how many defects were found by the end user after product delivery (D) in relation to the errors found before product delivery (E). The formula is:

DRE = E / (E+D)

The closer to 1 DRE is, the fewer defects found after product delivery.

With dozens of potential software metrics to track, it's crucial for development teams to evaluate their needs and select metrics that are aligned with business goals, relevant to the project, and represent valid measures of progress. Monitoring the right metrics (as opposed to not monitoring metrics at all or monitoring metrics that don't really matter) can mean the difference between a highly efficient, productive team and a floundering one. The same is true of software testing: using the right tests to evaluate the right features and functions is the key to success. (Check out our guide on software testing to learn more about the various testing types.)

While the process of defining goals, selecting metrics, and implementing consistent measurement methods can be time-consuming, the productivity gains and time saved over the life of a project make it time well invested. Various software metrics are incorporated into solutions such as application performance management (APM) tools, along with data and insights on application usage, code performance, slow requests, and much more. Retrace, Stackify's APM solution, combines APM, logs, errors, monitoring, and metrics in one, providing a fully-integrated, multi-environment application performance solution to level-up your development work. Check out Stackify's interview with John Sumser with HR Examiner, and one of Forbes Magazine's 20 to Watch in Big Data, for more insights on DevOps and Big Data.

Types of Software Metrics

Software metrics can be classified into two types as follows:

1. Product Metrics: These are the measures of various characteristics of the software product. The two important software characteristics are:

       1.   Size and complexity of software.
       2.   Quality and reliability of software.

These metrics can be computed for different stages of SDLC.

2. Process Metrics: These are the measures of various characteristics of the software development process. For example, the efficiency of fault detection. They are used to measure the characteristics of methods, techniques, and tools that are used for developing software.

Classification of Software Metrics

Types of Metrics

Internal metrics: Internal metrics are the metrics used for measuring properties that are viewed to be of greater importance to a software developer. For example, Lines of Code (LOC) measure.

External metrics: External metrics are the metrics used for measuring properties that are viewed to be of greater importance to the user, e.g., portability, reliability, functionality, usability, etc.

Hybrid metrics: Hybrid metrics are the metrics that combine product, process, and resource metrics. For example, cost per FP where FP stands for Function Point Metric.

Project metrics: Project metrics are the metrics used by the project manager to check the project's progress. Data from the past projects are used to collect various metrics, like time and cost; these estimates are used as a base of new software. Note that as the project proceeds, the project manager will check its progress from time-to-time and will compare the effort, cost, and time with the original effort, cost and time. Also understand that these metrics are used to decrease the development costs, time efforts and risks. The project quality can also be improved. As quality improves, the number of errors and time, as well as cost required, is also reduced.

Advantage of Software Metrics

- Comparative study of various design methodology of software systems.
- For analysis, comparison, and critical study of different programming language concerning their characteristics.

- In comparing and evaluating the capabilities and productivity of people involved in software development.
  - In the preparation of software quality specifications.
- In the verification of compliance of software systems requirements and specifications.
  - In making inference about the effort to be put in the design and development of the software systems.
  - In getting an idea about the complexity of the code.
- In taking decisions regarding further division of a complex module is to be done or not.
  - In guiding resource manager for their proper utilization.
  - In comparison and making design tradeoffs between software development and maintenance cost.
- In providing feedback to software managers about the progress and quality during various phases of the software development life cycle
  - In the allocation of testing resources for testing the code.

Disadvantage of Software Metrics

- The application of software metrics is not always easy, and in some cases, it is difficult and costly.
- The verification and justification of software metrics are based on historical/empirical data whose validity is difficult to verify.
- These are useful for managing software products but not for evaluating the performance of the technical staff.
- The definition and derivation of Software metrics are usually based on assuming which are not standardized and may depend upon tools available and working environment.
- Most of the predictive models rely on estimates of certain variables which are often not known precisely.

Software Quality Attributes

Software Quality Attributes are: Correctness, Reliability, Adequacy, Learnability, Robustness, Maintainability, Readability, Extensibility, Testability, Efficiency, Portability.

Correctness: The correctness of a software system refers to:

- Agreement of program code with specifications
- Independence of the actual application of the software system.

The **correctness** of a program becomes especially critical when it is embedded in a complex software system.

Reliability: Reliability of a software system derives from

- Correctness
- Availability

The behavior over time for the fulfillment of a given specification depends on the reliability of the software system.

Reliability of a software system is defined as the probability that this system fulfills a function (determined by the specifications) for a specified number of input trials under specified input conditions in a specified time interval (assuming that hardware and input are free of errors).

A software system can be seen as reliable if this test produces a low error rate (i.e., the probability that an error will occur in a specified time interval.)

The error rate depends on the frequency of inputs and on the probability that an individual input will lead to an error.

Adequacy: Factors for the requirement of Adequacy:

- The input required of the user should be limited to only what is necessary. The software system should expect information only if it is necessary for the functions that the user wishes to carry out. The software system should enable flexible data input on the part of the user and should carry out plausibility checks on the input. In dialog-driven software systems, we vest particular importance in the uniformity, clarity and simplicity of the dialogs.

- The performance offered by the software system should be adapted to the wishes of the user with the consideration given to extensibility; i.e., the functions should be limited to these in the specification.

- **The results produced by the software system:** The results that a software system delivers should be output in a clear and wellstructured form and be easy to interpret. The software system should afford the user flexibility with respect to the scope, the degree of detail, and the form of presentation of the results. Error messages must be provided in a form that is comprehensible for the user.

Learnability: Learnability of a software system depends on:

- The design of user interfaces
- The clarity and the simplicity of the user instructions

The user interface should present information as close to reality as possible and permit efficient utilization of the software's failures.

The user manual should be structured clearly and simply and be free of all dead weight. It should explain to the user what the software system should do, how the individual functions are activated, what relationships exist between functions, and which exceptions might arise and how they can be corrected. In addition, the user manual should serve as a reference that supports the user in quickly and comfortably finding the correct answers to questions.

Robustness: Robustness reduces the impact of operational mistakes, erroneous input data, and hardware errors.

A software system is robust if the consequences of an error in its operation, in the input, or in the hardware, in relation to a given application, are inversely proportional to the probability of the occurrence of this error in the given application.

- Frequent errors (e.g. erroneous commands, typing errors) must be handled with particular care.

- Less frequent errors (e.g. power failure) can be handled more laxly, but still must not lead to irreversible consequences.

Maintainability: Maintainability = suitability for debugging (localization and correction of errors) and for modification and extension of functionality.

The **maintainability** of a software system depends on its:

- Readability
- Extensibility
- Testability

Readability: Readability of a software system depends on its:

- Form of representation
- Programming style
- Consistency
- Readability of the implementation programming languages
- Structuredness of the system
- Quality of the documentation
- Tools available for inspection

Extensibility: Extensibility allows required modifications at the appropriate locations to be made without undesirable side effects. Extensibility of a software system depends on its:

- Structuredness (modularity) of the software system
- Possibilities that the implementation language provides for this purpose
- Readability (to find the appropriate location) of the code

- Availability of comprehensible program documentation

Testability: suitability for allowing the programmer to follow program execution (runtime behavior under given conditions) and for debugging. The testability of a software system depends on its:

- Modularity
- Structuredness

Modular, well-structured programs prove more suitable for systematic, stepwise testing than monolithic, unstructured programs.

Testing tools and the possibility of formulating consistency conditions (assertions) in the source code reduce the testing effort and provide important prerequisites for the extensive, systematic testing of all system components.

Efficiency: ability of a software system to fulfill its purpose with the best possible utilization of all necessary resources (time, storage, transmission channels, and peripherals).

Portability: the ease with which a software system can be adapted to run on computers other than the one for which it was designed.

The portability of a software system depends on:

- Degree of hardware independence
- Implementation language
- Extent of exploitation of specialized system functions
- Hardware properties
- Structuredness: System-dependent elements are collected in easily interchangeable program components.

A software system can be said to be portable if the effort required for porting it proves significantly less than the effort necessary for a new implementation.

CHAPTER FOUR

Cyclomatic Complexity

Cyclomatic complexity of a code section is the quantitative measure of the number of linearly independent paths in it. It is a software metric used to indicate the complexity of a program. It is computed using the Control Flow Graph of the program. The nodes in the graph indicate the smallest group of commands of a program, and a directed edge in it connects the two nodes I.e. If second command might immediately follow the first command.

For example, if source code contains no control flow statement then its cyclomatic complexity will be 1 and source code contains a single path in it. Similarly, if the source code contains one **if condition** then cyclomatic complexity will be 2 because there will be two paths one for true and the other for false.

Mathematically, for a structured program, the directed graph inside control flow is the edge joining two basic blocks of the program as control may pass from first to second.

So, cyclomatic complexity M would be defined as,

$M = E - N + 2P$

where,

E = *the number of edges in the control flow graph*

N = *the number of nodes in the control flow graph*

P = *the number of connected components*

Steps that should be followed in calculating cyclomatic complexity and test cases design are:

- Construction of graph with nodes and edges from code.
- Identification of independent paths.

- Cyclomatic Complexity Calculation
- Design of Test Cases

Let a section of code as such:
A = 10
IF B > C THEN
A = B
ELSE
A = C
ENDIF
Print A Print B Print C

Control Flow Graph of above code

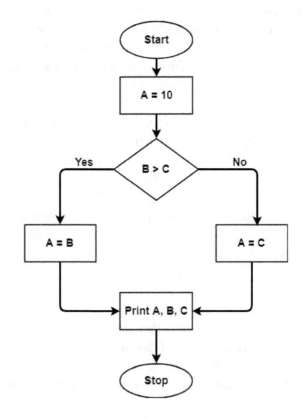

The cyclomatic complexity calculated for above code will be from control flow graph. The graph shows seven shapes(nodes), seven lines(edges), hence cyclomatic complexity is 7-7+2 = 2.

Use of Cyclomatic Complexity:

- Determining the independent path executions thus proven to be very helpful for Developers and Testers.
- It can make sure that every path have been tested at least once.
- Thus help to focus more on uncovered paths.
- Code coverage can be improved.
- Risk associated with program can be evaluated.
- These metrics being used earlier in the program helps in reducing the risks.

Software Requirements Analysis

Software requirement is a functional or non-functional need to be implemented in the system. Functional means providing particular service to the user.

For example, in context to banking application the functional requirement will be when customer selects "View Balance" they must be able to look at their latest account balance.

Software requirement can also be a non-functional, it can be a performance requirement. For example, a non-functional requirement is where every page of the system should be visible to the users within 5 seconds.

So, basically **software requirement is a**

- Functional or
- Non-functional

need that has to be implemented into the system. **Software requirement are usually expressed as a statements.**

- Types of Requirements
- Other Sources of Requirements
- How to Analyze Requirements
- Atomic
- Uniquely Identified
- Complete
- Consistent and Unambiguous
- Traceable
- Prioritized
- Testable
- Conclusion

Types of Requirements

1. **Business requirements**: They are high-level requirements that are taken from the business case from the projects.

2. **Architectural and Design requirements**: These requirements are more detailed than business requirements. It determines the overall design required to implement the business requirement.
3. **System and Integration requirements**: At the lowest level, we have system and integration requirements. It is detailed description of each and every requirement. It can be in form of user stories which is really describing everyday business language. The requirements are in abundant details so that developers can begin coding.

Other Sources of Requirements

- Knowledge transfer from colleagues or employees already working on that project
- Talk about project to business analyst, product manager, project lead and developers
- Analyze previous system version that is already implemented into the system
- Analyze the older requirement document of the project
- Look into the past Bug reports, some of the bug reports are turned into enhancement request which may be implemented into current version
- Look into installation guide if it is available to see what are the installation required
- Analyze the domain or industry knowledge that team is trying to implement

Whatever source of requirement you get make sure to document them in some form, get them reviewed from other experienced and knowledgeable team members.

How to Analyze Requirements

Consider example of an educational software system where a student can register for different courses.

Lets study how to analyze the requirements. The requirements must maintain a standard quality of its requirement, different types of requirement quality includes

- Atomic
- Uniquely identified
- Complete
- Consistent and unambiguous
- Traceable
- Prioritized
- Testable

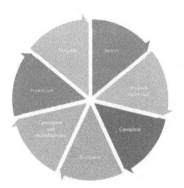

Requirements Analysis

Requirement analysis is significant and essential activity after elicitation. We analyze, refine, and scrutinize the gathered requirements to make consistent and unambiguous requirements. This activity reviews all requirements and may provide a graphical view of the entire system. After the completion of the analysis, it is expected that the understandability of the project may improve significantly. Here, we may also use the interaction with the customer to clarify points of confusion and to understand which requirements are more important than others.

The various steps of requirement analysis are shown in fig:

(i) Draw the context diagram: The context diagram is a simple model that defines the boundaries and interfaces of the proposed systems with the external world. It identifies the entities outside the proposed system that interact with the system. The context diagram of student result management system is given below:

(ii) Development of a Prototype (optional): One effective way to find out what the customer wants is to construct a prototype, something that looks and preferably acts as part of the system they say they want.

We can use their feedback to modify the prototype until the customer is satisfied continuously. Hence, the prototype helps the client to visualize the proposed system and increase the understanding of the requirements. When developers and users are not sure about some of the elements, a prototype may help both the parties to take a final decision.

Some projects are developed for the general market. In such cases, the prototype should be shown to some representative sample of the population of potential purchasers. Even though a person who tries out a prototype may not buy the final system, but their feedback may allow us to make the product more attractive to others.

The prototype should be built quickly and at a relatively low cost. Hence it will always have limitations and would not be acceptable in the final system. This is an optional activity.

(iii) Model the requirements: This process usually consists of various graphical representations of the functions, data entities, external entities, and the relationships between them. The graphical view may help to find incorrect, inconsistent, missing, and superfluous requirements. Such models include the Data Flow diagram, Entity-Relationship diagram, Data Dictionaries, State-transition diagrams, etc.

(iv) Finalise the requirements: After modeling the requirements, we will have a better understanding of the system behavior. The inconsistencies and ambiguities have been identified and corrected. The flow of data amongst various modules has been analyzed. Elicitation and analyze activities have provided better insight into the system. Now we finalize the analyzed requirements, and the next step is to document these requirements in a prescribed format.

CHAPTER FIVE

SOFTWARE REQUIREMENT SPECIFICATION (SRS)

A **software requirements specification** (SRS) is a detailed description of a software system to be developed with its functional and non-functional requirements. The SRS is developed based the agreement between customer and contractors. It may include the use cases of how user is going to interact with software system. The software requirement specification document consistent of all necessary requirements required for project development. To develop the software system we should have clear understanding of Software system. To achieve this we need to continuous communication with customers to gather all requirements.

A good SRS defines the how Software System will interact with all internal modules, hardware, communication with other programs and human user interactions with wide range of real life scenarios. Using the *Software requirements specification* (SRS) document on QA lead, managers creates test plan. It is very important that testers must be cleared with every detail specified in this document in order to avoid faults in test cases and its expected results.

It is highly recommended to review or test SRS documents before start writing test cases and making any plan for testing. Let's see how to test SRS and the important point to keep in mind while testing it.

1. Correctness of SRS should be checked. Since the whole testing phase is dependent on SRS, it is very important to check its correctness. There are some standards with which we can compare and verify.

2. Ambiguity should be avoided. Sometimes in SRS, some words have more than one meaning and this might confused testers making it difficult to get the exact reference. It is advisable to check for such ambiguous words and make the meaning clear for better understanding.

3. Requirements should be complete. When tester writes test cases, what exactly is required from the application, is the first thing which needs to be clear. For e.g. if application needs to send the specific data of some specific size then it should be clearly mentioned in SRS that how much data and what is the size limit to send.

4. Consistent requirements. The SRS should be consistent within itself and consistent to its reference documents. If you call an input "Start and Stop" in one place, don't call it "Start/Stop" in another. This sets the standard and should be followed throughout the testing phase.

5. Verification of expected result: SRS should not have statements like "Work as expected", it should be clearly stated that what is expected since different testers would have different thinking aspects and may draw different results from this statement.

6. Testing environment: some applications need specific conditions to test and also a particular environment for accurate result. SRS should have clear documentation on what type of environment is needed to set up.

7. Pre-conditions defined clearly: one of the most important part of test cases is pre-conditions. If they are not met properly then actual result will always be different expected result. Verify that in SRS, all the pre-conditions are mentioned clearly.

8. Requirements ID: these are the base of test case template. Based on requirement Ids, test case ids are written. Also, requirements ids make it easy to categorize modules so just by looking at them, tester will know which module to refer. SRS must have them such as id defines a particular module.

9. Security and Performance criteria: security is priority when a software is tested especially when it is built in such a way that it contains some crucial information when leaked can cause harm to business. Tester should check that all the security related requirements are properly defined and are clear to him. Also, when we talk about performance of a software, it plays a very important role in business so all the requirements related to performance must be clear to the tester and he must also know when and how much stress or load testing should be done to test the performance.

10. Assumption should be avoided: sometimes when requirement is not cleared to tester, he tends to make some assumptions related to it, which is not a right way to do testing as assumptions could go wrong and hence, test results may vary. It is better to avoid assumptions and ask clients about all the "missing requirements" to have a better understanding of expected results.

11. Deletion of irrelevant requirements: there are more than one team who work on SRS so it might be possible that some irrelevant requirements are included in SRS. Based on the understanding of the software, tester can find out which are these requirements and remove them to avoid confusions and reduce work load.

12. Freeze requirements: when an ambiguous or incomplete requirement is sent to client to analyze and tester gets a reply, that requirement result will be updated in the next SRS version and client will freeze that requirement. Freezing here means that result will not change again until and unless some major addition or modification is introduced in the software

Data Flow Diagrams

A Data Flow Diagram (DFD) is a traditional visual representation of the information flows within a system. A neat and clear DFD can depict the right amount of the system requirement graphically. It can be manual, automated, or a combination of both.

It shows how data enters and leaves the system, what changes the information, and where data is stored.

The objective of a DFD is to show the scope and boundaries of a system as a whole. It may be used as a communication tool between a system analyst and any person who plays a part in the order that acts as a starting point for redesigning a system. The DFD is also called as a data flow graph or bubble chart.

The following observations about DFDs are essential:

1. All names should be unique. This makes it easier to refer to elements in the DFD.
2. Remember that DFD is not a flow chart. Arrows is a flow chart that represents the order of events; arrows in DFD represents flowing data. A DFD does not involve any order of events.
3. Suppress logical decisions. If we ever have the urge to draw a diamond-shaped box in a DFD, suppress that urge! A diamond-shaped box is used in flow charts to represents decision points with multiple exists paths of which the only one is taken. This implies an ordering of events, which makes no sense in a DFD.
4. Do not become bogged down with details. Defer error conditions and error handling until the end of the analysis.

Standard symbols for DFDs are derived from the electric circuit diagram analysis and are shown in fig:

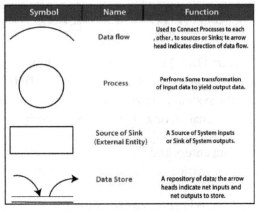

Symbol	Name	Function
	Data flow	Used to Connect Processes to each other, to sources or Sinks; te arrow head indicates direction of data flow.
	Process	Perfroms Some transformation of Input data to yield output data.
	Source of Sink (External Entity)	A Source of System inputs or Sink of System outputs.
	Data Store	A repository of data; the arrow heads indicate net inputs and net outputs to store.

Symbols for Data Flow Diagrams

Circle: A circle (bubble) shows a process that transforms data inputs into data outputs.

Data Flow: A curved line shows the flow of data into or out of a process or data store.

Data Store: A set of parallel lines shows a place for the collection of data items. A data store indicates that the data is stored which can be used at a later stage or by the other processes in a different order. The data store can have an element or group of elements.

Source or Sink: Source or Sink is an external entity and acts as a source of system inputs or sink of system outputs.

Advantages of data flow diagram:

- It aids in describing the boundaries of the system.

- It is beneficial for communicating existing system knowledge to the users.
- A straightforward graphical technique which is easy to recognise.
- DFDs can provide a detailed representation of system components.
- It is used as the part of system documentation file.
- DFDs are easier to understand by technical and nontechnical audiences
- It supports the logic behind the data flow within the system

Disadvantages of data flow diagram:

- It make the programmers little confusing concerning the system.
- The biggest drawback of the DFD is that it simply takes a long time to create, so long that the analyst may not receive support from management to complete it.
- Physical considerations are left out.

Levels in DFD

The DFD may be used to perform a system or software at any level of abstraction. Infact, DFDs may be partitioned into levels that represent increasing information flow and functional detail. Levels in DFD are numbered 0, 1, 2 or beyond. Here, we will see primarily three levels in the data flow diagram, which are: 0-level DFD, 1-level DFD, and 2-level DFD.

0-level DFDM

It is also known as fundamental system model, or context diagram represents the entire software requirement as a single bubble with input and output data denoted by incoming and outgoing arrows. Then the system is decomposed and described as a DFD with multiple bubbles. Parts of the system represented by each of these bubbles are then decomposed and documented as more and more detailed DFDs. This process may be repeated at as many levels as necessary until the program at hand is well understood. It is essential to preserve the number of inputs and outputs between levels, this concept is called leveling by DeMacro. Thus, if bubble "A" has two inputs x_1 and x_2 and one output y, then the expanded DFD, that represents "A" should have exactly two external inputs and one external output as shown in fig:

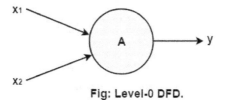

Fig: Level-0 DFD.

The Level-0 DFD, also called context diagram of the result management system is shown in fig. As the bubbles are decomposed into less and less abstract bubbles, the corresponding data flow may also be needed to be decomposed.

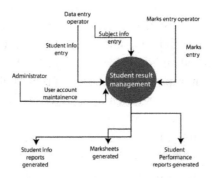

Fig: Level-0 DFD of result management system

1-level DFD

In 1-level DFD, a context diagram is decomposed into multiple bubbles/ processes. In this level, we highlight the main objectives of the system and breakdown the high-level process of 0-level DFD into subprocesses.

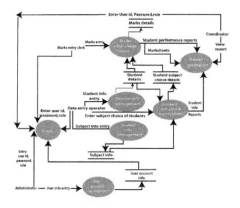

Fig: Level-1 DFD of result management system

2-Level DFD

2-level DFD goes one process deeper into parts of 1-level DFD. It can be used to project or record the specific/necessary detail about the system's functioning.

1.User Account Maintenance

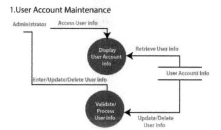

2. Login

The level 2 DFD of this process is given below:

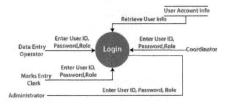

3. Student Information Management

4. Subject Information Management

The level 2 DFD of this process is given below:

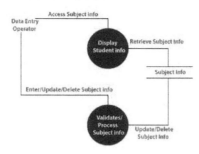

5. Student's Subject Choice Management

The Level 2 DFD of this Process is given below:

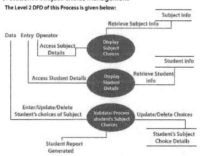

6. Marks Information Managment

The Level 2 DFO of this Process is given below:

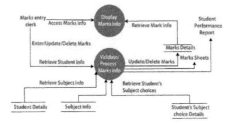

Data dictionary

A data dictionary is a file or a set of files that includes a database's metadata. The data dictionary hold records about other objects in the database, such as data ownership, data relationships to other objects, and other data. The data dictionary is an essential component of any relational database. Ironically, because of its importance, it is invisible to most database users. Typically, only database administrators interact with the data dictionary.

The data dictionary, in general, includes information about the following:

- Name of the data item
- Aliases
- Description/purpose
- Related data items
- Range of values
- Data structure definition/Forms

The **name of the data item** is self-explanatory.

Aliases include other names by which this data item is called DEO for Data Entry Operator and DR for Deputy Registrar.

Description/purpose is a textual description of what the data item is used for or why it exists.

Related data items capture relationships between data items e.g., total_marks must always equal to internal_marks plus external_marks.

Range of values records all possible values, e.g. total marks must be positive and between 0 to 100.

Data structure Forms: Data flows capture the name of processes that generate or receive the data items. If the data item is primitive, then data structure form captures the physical structures of the data item. If the data is itself a data aggregate, then data structure form capture the composition of the data items in terms of other data items.

The mathematical operators used within the data dictionary are defined in the table:

Notations	Meaning
x=a+b	x includes of data elements a and b.
x=[a/b]	x includes of either data elements a or b.
x=a x	includes of optimal data elements a.
x=y[a]	x includes of y or more occurrences of data element a
x=[a]z	x includes of z or fewer occurrences of data element a
x=y[a]z	x includes of some occurrences of data element a which are between y and z.

The data dictionary can be used to

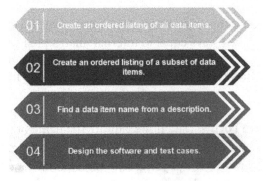

01 Create an ordered listing of all data items.

02 Create an ordered listing of a subset of data items.

03 Find a data item name from a description.

04 Design the software and test cases.

Advantage and Disadvantages of Data Dictionary

Advantage of Data Dictionary

- There is lot of advantages of data dictionary. Some of main points are
- It gives the well structured and clear information about the database. One can analyze the requirement, any redundancy like duplicate columns, tables etc. Since it provides a good documentation on each object, it helps to understand the requirement and design to the great extent.
- It is very helpful for the administrator or any new DBA to understand the database. Since it has all the information about the database, DBA can easily able to track any chaos in the database.
- Since database is a very huge, and will have lots of tables, views, constraints, indexes etc, it will be difficult for anyone to remember. Data dictionary helps user by providing all the details in it.

Disadvantages of Data Dictionary

- Creating a new data dictionary is a very big task. It will take years to create one.
- It should be well designed in advance to take all the advantages of it. Otherwise, it will create problems throughout its life.
- The cost of data dictionary will be bit high as it includes its initial build and hardware charges as well as cost of maintenance.
- Non technical users will not understand what the columns in the data dictionary views are. It meant only for technical users.

Entity-Relationship Diagrams

ER-modeling is a data modeling method used in software engineering to produce a conceptual data model of an information system. Diagrams created using this ER-modeling method are called Entity-Relationship Diagrams or ER diagrams or ERDs.

Purpose of ERD

The database analyst gains a better understanding of the data to be contained in the database through the step of constructing the ERD.

The ERD serves as a documentation tool.

Finally, the ERD is used to connect the logical structure of the database to users. In particular, the ERD effectively communicates the logic of the database to users.

Components of an ER Diagrams

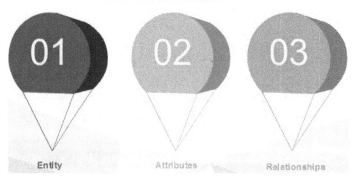

Components of a ER Diagram

01 Entity

02 Attributes

03 Relationships

1. Entity

An entity can be a real-world object, either animate or inanimate, that can be merely identifiable. An entity is denoted as a rectangle in an ER diagram. For example, in a school database, students, teachers, classes, and courses offered can be treated as entities. All these entities have some attributes or properties that give them their identity.

Entity Set

An entity set is a collection of related types of entities. An entity set may include entities with attribute sharing similar values. For example, a Student set may contain all the students of a school; likewise, a Teacher set may include all the teachers of a school from all faculties. Entity set need not be disjoint.

2. Attributes

Entities are denoted utilizing their properties, known as attributes. All attributes have values. For example, a student entity may have name, class, and age as attributes.

There exists a domain or range of values that can be assigned to attributes. For example, a student's name cannot be a numeric value. It has to be alphabetic. A student's age cannot be negative, etc.

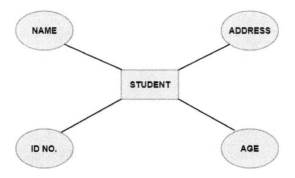

There are four types of Attributes:

1. Key attribute
2. Composite attribute
3. Single-valued attribute
4. Multi-valued attribute
5. Derived attribute

1. Key attribute: Key is an attribute or collection of attributes that uniquely identifies an entity among the entity set. For example, the roll_number of a student makes him identifiable among students.

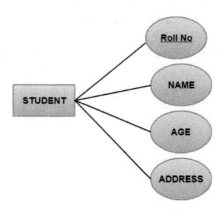

There are mainly three types of keys:

1. **Super key:** A set of attributes that collectively identifies an entity in the entity set.
2. **Candidate key:** A minimal super key is known as a candidate key. An entity set may have more than one candidate key.

3. **Primary key:** A primary key is one of the candidate keys chosen by the database designer to uniquely identify the entity set.

2. Composite attribute: An attribute that is a combination of other attributes is called a composite attribute. For example, In student entity, the student address is a composite attribute as an address is composed of other characteristics such as pin code, state, country.

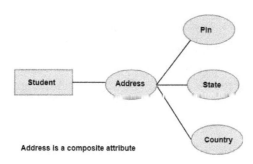

Address is a composite attribute

3. Single-valued attribute: Single-valued attribute contain a single value. For example, Social_Security_Number.

4. Multi-valued Attribute: If an attribute can have more than one value, it is known as a multi-valued attribute. Multi-valued attributes are depicted by the double ellipse. For example, a person can have more than one phone number, email-address, etc.

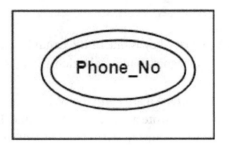

5. Derived attribute: Derived attributes are the attribute that does not exist in the physical database, but their values are derived from other attributes present in the database. For example, age can be derived from date_of_birth. In the ER diagram, Derived attributes are depicted by the dashed ellipse.

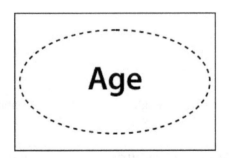

The Complete entity type Student with its attributes can be represented as:

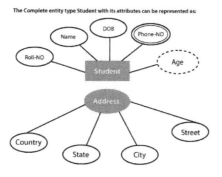

3. Relationships

The association among entities is known as relationship. Relationships are represented by the diamond-shaped box. For example, an employee works_at a department, a student enrolls in a course. Here, Works_at and Enrolls are called relationships.

Fig: Relationships in ERD

Relationship set

A set of relationships of a similar type is known as a relationship set. Like entities, a relationship too can have attributes. These attributes are called descriptive attributes.

Degree of a relationship set

The number of participating entities in a relationship describes the degree of the relationship. The three most common relationships in E-R models are:

1. Unary (degree1)
2. Binary (degree2)
3. Ternary (degree3)

1. Unary relationship: This is also called recursive relationships. It is a relationship between the instances of one entity type. For example, one person is married to only one person.

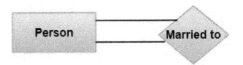

Fig: Unary Relationship

2. Binary relationship: It is a relationship between the instances of two entity types. For example, the Teacher teaches the subject.

Fig: Binary Relationship

3. Ternary relationship: It is a relationship amongst instances of three entity types. In fig, the relationships "**may have**" provide the association of three entities, i.e., TEACHER, STUDENT, and SUBJECT. All three entities are many-to-many participants. There may be one or many participants in a ternary relationship.

In general, "**n**" entities can be related by the same relationship and is known as **n-ary** relationship.

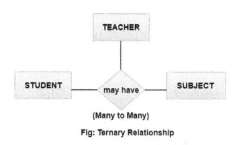

(Many to Many)

Fig: Ternary Relationship

Cardinality

Cardinality describes the number of entities in one entity set, which can be associated with the number of entities of other sets via relationship set.

Types of Cardinalities

1. One to One: One entity from entity set A can be contained with at most one entity of entity set B and vice versa. Let us assume that each student has only one student ID, and each student ID is assigned to only one person. So, the relationship will be one to one.

Using Sets, it can be represented as:

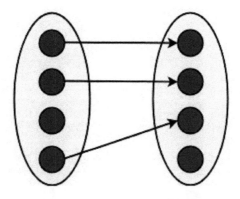

2. One to many: When a single instance of an entity is associated with more than one instances of another entity then it is called one to many relationships. For example, a client can place many orders; a order cannot be placed by many customers.

Using Sets, it can be represented as:

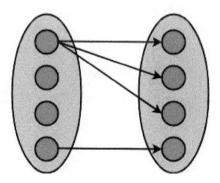

3. Many to One: More than one entity from entity set A can be associated with at most one entity of entity set B, however an entity from entity set B can be associated with more than one entity from entity set A. For example - many students can study in a single college, but a student cannot study in many colleges at the same time.

Using Sets, it can be represented as:

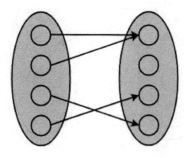

4. Many to Many: One entity from A can be associated with more than one entity from B and vice-versa. For example, the student can be assigned to many projects, and a project can be assigned to many students.

Using Sets, it can be represented as:

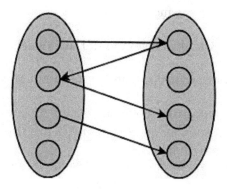

Advantages and Disadvantages of E-R Data Model

Following are advantages of an E-R Model:

• Straightforward relation representation: Having designed an E-R diagram for a database application, the relational representation of the database model becomes relatively straightforward.

• Easy conversion for E-R to other data model: Conversion from E-R diagram to a network or hierarchical data model can· easily be accomplished.

• Graphical representation for better understanding: An E-R model gives graphical and diagrammatical representation of various entities, its attributes and relationships between entities. This is turn helps in the clear understanding of the data structure and in minimizing redundancy and other problems.

Disadvantages of E-R Data Model

Following are disadvantages of an E-R Model:

• No industry standard for notation: There is no industry standard notation for developing an E-R diagram.

• Popular for high-level design: The E-R data model is especially popular for high level.

Quality Characteristics of a good SRS

Following are the characteristics of a good SRS document:

1. Correctness:
User review is used to ensure the correctness of requirements stated in the SRS. SRS is said to be correct if it covers all the requirements that are actually expected from the system.

2. Completeness:
Completeness of SRS indicates every sense of completion including the numbering of all the pages, resolving the to be determined parts to as much extent as possible as well as covering all the functional and non-functional requirements properly.

3. Consistency:
Requirements in SRS are said to be consistent if there are no conflicts between any set of requirements. Examples of conflict include differences in terminologies used at separate places, logical conflicts like time period of report generation, etc.

4. Unambiguousness:
An SRS is said to be unambiguous if all the requirements stated have only 1 interpretation. Some of the ways to prevent unambiguousness include the use of modelling techniques like ER diagrams, proper reviews and buddy checks, etc.

5. Ranking for importance and stability:
There should a criterion to classify the requirements as less or more important or more specifically as desirable or essential. An identifier mark can be used with every requirement to indicate its rank or stability.

6. Modifiability:
SRS should be made as modifiable as possible and should be capable of easily accepting changes to the system to some extent. Modifications should be properly indexed and cross-referenced.

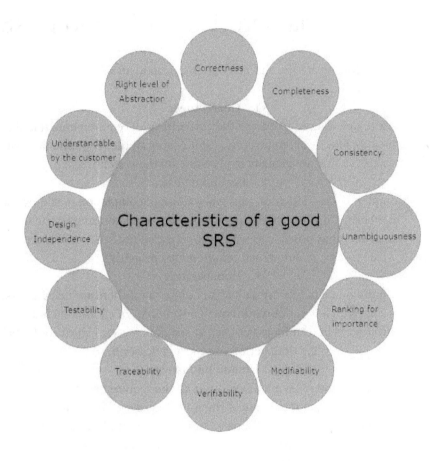

Characteristics of a good SRS

- Correctness
- Completeness
- Consistency
- Unambiguousness
- Ranking for importance
- Modifiability
- Verifiability
- Traceability
- Testability
- Design Independence
- Understandable by the customer
- Right level of Abstraction

8. Verifiability:

An SRS is verifiable if there exists a specific technique to quantifiably measure the extent to which every requirement is met by the system. For example, a requirement stating that the system must be user-friendly is not verifiable and listing such requirements should be avoided.

9. Traceability:

One should be able to trace a requirement to a design component and then to a code segment in the program. Similarly, one should be able to trace a requirement to the corresponding test cases.

10. Design Independence:

There should be an option to choose from multiple design alternatives for the final system. More specifically, the SRS should not include any implementation details.

11 Testability:

An SRS should be written in such a way that it is easy to generate test cases and test plans from the document.

12. Understandable by the customer:

An end user maybe an expert in his/her specific domain but might not be an expert in computer science. Hence, the use of formal notations and symbols should be avoided to as much extent as possible. The language should be kept easy and clear.

13. Right level of abstraction:

If the SRS is written for the requirements phase, the details should be explained explicitly. Whereas, for a feasibility study, fewer details can be used. Hence, the level of abstraction varies according to the purpose of the SRS.

Verification and Validation

Verification and Validation is the process of investigating that a software system satisfies specifications and standards and it fulfills the required purpose. **Barry Boehm** described verification and validation as the following:

Verification: Are we building the product right?
Validation: Are we building the right product?

Verification:

Verification is the process of checking that a software achieves its goal without any bugs. It is the process to ensure whether the product that is developed is right or not. It verifies whether the developed product fulfills the requirements that we have.
Verification is **Static Testing**.

Activities involved in verification:

1. Inspections
2. Reviews
3. Walkthroughs
4. Desk-checking

Validation:

Validation is the process of checking whether the software product is up to the mark or in other words product has high level requirements. It is the process of checking the validation of product i.e. it checks what we are developing is the right product. it is validation of actual and expected product.
Validation is the **Dynamic Testing**.

Activities involved in validation:

1. Black box testing
2. White box testing

3. Unit testing
4. Integration testing

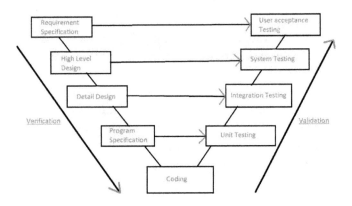

Note: Verification is followed by Validation.

CHAPTER SIX

SOFTWARE DESIGN

Once the requirements document for the software to be developed is available, the software design phase begins. While the requirement specification activity deals entirely with the problem domain, design is the first phase of transforming the problem into a solution. In the design phase, the customer and business requirements and technical considerations all come together to formulate a product or a system.

The design process comprises a set of principles, concepts and practices, which allow a software engineer to model the system or product that is to be built. This model, known as design model, is assessed for quality and reviewed before a code is generated and tests are conducted. The design model provides details about software data structures, architecture, interfaces and components which are required to implement the system. This chapter discusses the design elements that are required to develop a software design model. It also discusses the design patterns and various software design notations used to represent a software design.

Basic of Software Design

Software design is a phase in software engineering, in which a blueprint is developed to serve as a base for constructing the software system. **IEEE** defines software design as 'both a process of defining, the architecture, components, interfaces, and other characteristics of a system or component and the result of that process.'

In the design phase, many critical and strategic decisions are made to achieve the desired functionality and quality of the system. These decisions are taken into account to successfully develop the software and carry out its maintenance in a way that the quality of the end product is improved.

Principles of Software Design

Developing design is a cumbersome process as most expansive errors are often introduced in this phase. Moreover, if these errors get unnoticed till later phases, it becomes more difficult to correct them. Therefore, a number of principles are followed while designing the software. These principles act as a framework for the designers to follow a good design practice.

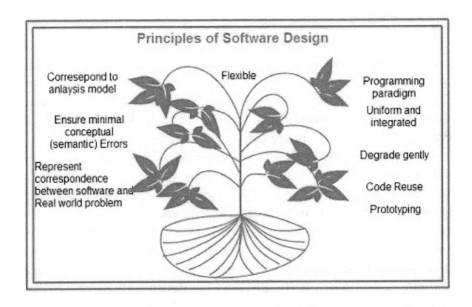

Some of the commonly followed design principles are as following.

1. **Software design should correspond to the analysis model:** Often a design element corresponds to many requirements, therefore, we must know how the design model satisfies all the requirements represented by the analysis model.

2. **Choose the right programming paradigm:** A programming paradigm describes the structure of the software system. Depending on the nature and type of application, different programming paradigms such as

procedure oriented, object-oriented, and prototyping paradigms can be used. The paradigm should be chosen keeping constraints in mind such as time, availability of resources and nature of user's requirements.

3. **Software design should be uniform and integrated:** Software design is considered uniform and integrated, if the interfaces are properly defined among the design components. For this, rules, format, and styles are established before the design team starts designing the software.

4. **Software design should be flexible:** Software design should be flexible enough to adapt changes easily. To achieve the flexibility, the basic design concepts such as abstraction, refinement, and modularity should be applied effectively.

5. **Software design should ensure minimal conceptual (semantic) errors:** The design team must ensure that major conceptual errors of design such as ambiguousness and inconsistency are addressed in advance before dealing with the syntactical errors present in the design model.

6. **Software design should be structured to degrade gently:** Software should be designed to handle unusual changes and circumstances, and if the need arises for termination, it must do so in a proper manner so that functionality of the software is not affected.

7. **Software design should represent correspondence between the software and real-world problem:** The software design should be structured in such away that it always relates with the real-world problem.

8. **Software reuse:** Software engineers believe on the phrase: 'do not reinvent the wheel'. Therefore, software components should be designed in such a way that they can be effectively reused to increase the productivity.

9. **Designing for testability:** A common practice that has been followed is to keep the testing phase separate from the design and implementation phases. That is, first the software is developed (designed and

implemented) and then handed over to the testers who subsequently determine whether the software is fit for distribution and subsequent use by the customer. However, it has become apparent that the process of separating testing is seriously flawed, as if any type of design or implementation errors are found after implementation, then the entire or a substantial part of the software requires to be redone. Thus, the test engineers should be involved from the initial stages. For example, they should be involved with analysts to prepare tests for determining whether the user requirements are being met.

10. **Prototyping:** Prototyping should be used when the requirements are not completely defined in the beginning. The user interacts with the developer to expand and refine the requirements as the development proceeds. Using prototyping, a quick 'mock-up' of the system can be developed. This mock-up can be used as a effective means to give the users a feel of what the system will look like and demonstrate functions that will be included in the developed system. Prototyping also helps in reducing risks of designing software that is not in accordance with the customer's requirements.

Note that design principles are often constrained by the existing hardware configuration, the implementation language, the existing file and data structures, and the existing organizational practices. Also, the evolution of each software design should be meticulously designed for future evaluations, references and maintenance.

Software Design Concepts

Every software process is characterized by basic concepts along with certain practices or methods. Methods represent the manner through which the concepts are applied. As new technology replaces older technology, many changes occur in the methods that are used to apply the concepts for the development of software. However, the fundamental concepts underlining the software design process remain the same, some of which are described here.

Abstraction

Abstraction refers to a powerful design tool, which allows software designers to consider components at an abstract level, while neglecting the implementation details of the components. **IEEE** defines abstraction as 'a view of a problem that extracts the essential information relevant to a particular purpose and ignores the remainder of the information.' The concept of abstraction can be used in two ways: as a process and as an entity. As a **process**, it refers to a mechanism of hiding irrelevant details and representing only the essential features of an item so that one can focus on important things at a time. As an **entity**, it refers to a model or view of an item.

Each step in the software process is accomplished through various levels of abstraction. At the highest level, an outline of the solution to the problem is presented whereas at the lower levels, the solution to the problem is presented in detail. For example, in the requirements analysis phase, a solution to the problem is presented using the language of problem environment and as we proceed through the software process, the abstraction level reduces and at the lowest level, source code of the software is produced.

There are three commonly used abstraction mechanisms in software design, namely, functional abstraction, data abstraction and control abstraction. All these mechanisms allow us to control the complexity of the design process by proceeding from the abstract design model to concrete design model in a systematic manner.

1. **Functional abstraction:** This involves the use of parameterized subprograms. Functional abstraction can be generalized as collections of subprograms referred to as 'groups'. Within these groups there exist routines which may be visible or hidden. Visible routines can be used within the containing groups as well as within other groups, whereas hidden routines are hidden from other groups and can be used within the containing group only.

2. **Data abstraction:** This involves specifying data that describes a data object. For example, the data object *window* encompasses a set of attributes (window type, window dimension) that describe the window object clearly. In this abstraction mechanism, representation and

manipulation details are ignored.

3. **Control abstraction:** This states the desired effect, without stating the exact mechanism of control. For example, if and while statements in programming languages (like C and C++) are abstractions of machine code implementations, which involve conditional instructions. In the architectural design level, this abstraction mechanism permits specifications of sequential subprogram and exception handlers without the concern for exact details of implementation.

Architecture

Software architecture refers to the structure of the system, which is composed of various components of a program/ system, the attributes (properties) of those components and the relationship amongst them. The software architecture enables the software engineers to analyze the software design efficiently. In addition, it also helps them in decision-making and handling risks. The software architecture does the following.

- Provides an insight to all the interested stakeholders that enable them to communicate with each other
- Highlights early design decisions, which have great impact on the software engineering activities (like coding and testing) that follow the design phase
- Creates intellectual models of how the system is organized into components and how these components interact with each other.

Currently, software architecture is represented in an informal and unplanned manner. Though the architectural concepts are often represented in the infrastructure (for supporting particular architectural styles) and the initial stages of a system configuration, the lack of an explicit independent characterization of architecture restricts the advantages of this design concept in the present scenario.

Note that software architecture comprises two elements of design model, namely, data design and architectural design.

Patterns

A pattern provides a description of the solution to a recurring design problem of some specific domain in such a way that the solution can be used again and again. The objective of each pattern is to provide an insight to a designer who can determine the following.

1. Whether the pattern can be reused
2. Whether the pattern is applicable to the current project
3. Whether the pattern can be used to develop a similar but functionally or structurally different design pattern.

Types of Design Patterns

Software engineer can use the design pattern during the entire software design process. When the analysis model is developed, the designer can examine the problem description at different levels of abstraction to determine whether it complies with one or more of the following types of design patterns.

1. **Architectural patterns:** These patterns are high-level strategies that refer to the overall structure and organization of a software system. That is, they define the elements of a software system such as subsystems, components, classes, etc. In addition, they also indicate the relationship between the elements along with the rules and guidelines for specifying these relationships. Note that architectural patterns are often considered equivalent to software architecture.

2. **Design patterns:** These patterns are medium-level strategies that are used to solve design problems. They provide a means for the refinement of the elements (as defined by architectural pattern) of a software system or the relationship among them. Specific design elements such as relationship among components or mechanisms that affect component-to-component interaction are addressed by design patterns. Note that design patterns are often considered equivalent to software components.

3. **Idioms:** These patterns are low-level patterns, which are programming-language specific. They describe the implementation of a software component, the method used for interaction among software

components, etc., in a specific programming language. Note that idioms are often termed as coding patterns.

Modularity

Modularity is achieved by dividing the software into uniquely named and addressable components, which are also known as **modules.** A complex system (large program) is partitioned into a set of discrete modules in such a way that each module can be developed independent of other modules. After developing the modules, they are integrated together to meet the software requirements. Note that larger the number of modules a system is divided into, greater will be the effort required to integrate the modules.

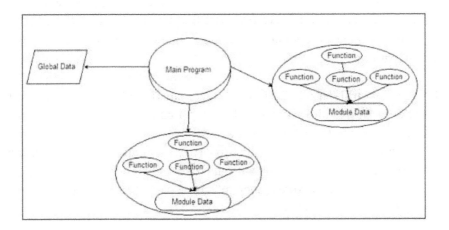

Modularizing a design helps to plan the development in a more effective manner, accommodate changes easily, conduct testing and debugging effectively and efficiently, and conduct maintenance work without adversely affecting the functioning of the software.

Information Hiding

Modules should be specified and designed in such a way that the data structures and processing details of one module are not accessible to other modules. They pass only that much information to each other, which is required to accomplish the software functions. The way of hiding unnecessary details is referred to as **information hiding.** **IEEE** defines information hiding as 'the technique of encapsulating software design decisions in modules in such a way that the module's interfaces reveal as little as possible about the module's inner workings; thus each module is a 'black box' to the other modules in the system.

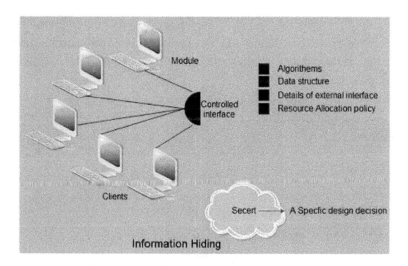

Information Hiding

Information hiding is of immense use when modifications are required during the testing and maintenance phase. Some of the advantages associated with information hiding are listed below.

1. Leads to low coupling
2. Emphasizes communication through controlled interfaces
3. Decreases the probability of adverse effects
4. Restricts the effects of changes in one component on others
5. Results in higher quality software.

Stepwise Refinement

Stepwise refinement is a top-down design strategy used for decomposing a system from a high level of abstraction into a more detailed level (lower level) of abstraction. At the highest level of abstraction, function or information is defined conceptually without providing any information about the internal workings of the function or internal structure of the data. As we proceed towards the lower levels of abstraction, more and more details are available.

Software designers start the stepwise refinement process by creating a sequence of compositions for the system being designed. Each composition is more detailed than the previous one and contains more components and interactions. The earlier compositions represent the significant interactions within the system, while the later compositions show in detail how these interactions are achieved.

To have a clear understanding of the concept, let us consider an example of stepwise refinement. Every computer program comprises input, process, and output.

1. INPUT

- Get user's name (string) through a prompt.
- Get user's grade (integer from 0 to 100) through a prompt and validate.

2. PROCESS
3. OUTPUT

This is the first step in refinement. The input phase can be refined further as given here.

1. INPUT

  ○ Get user's name through a prompt.
  ○ Get user's grade through a prompt.
  ○ While (invalid grade)

  Ask again:

2. PROCESS
3. OUTPUT

Note: Stepwise refinement can also be performed for PROCESS and OUTPUT phase.

Refactoring

Refactoring is an important design activity that reduces the complexity of module design keeping its behaviour or function unchanged. Refactoring can be defined as a process of modifying a software system to improve the internal structure of design without changing its external behavior. During the refactoring process, the existing design is checked for any type of flaws like redundancy, poorly constructed algorithms and data structures, etc., in order to improve the design. For example, a design model might yield a component which exhibits low cohesion (like a component performs four functions that have a limited relationship with one another). Software designers may decide to refactor the component into four different components, each exhibiting high cohesion. This leads to easier integration, testing, and maintenance of the software components.

Structural Partitioning

When the architectural style of a design follows a hierarchical nature, the structure of the program can be partitioned either horizontally or vertically. In **horizontal partitioning,** the control modules are used to communicate between functions and execute the functions. Structural partitioning provides the following benefits.

- The testing and maintenance of software becomes easier.
- The negative impacts spread slowly.
- The software can be extended easily.

Besides these advantages, horizontal partitioning has some disadvantage also. It requires to pass more data across the module interface, which makes the control flow of the problem more complex. This usually happens in cases where data moves rapidly from one function to another.

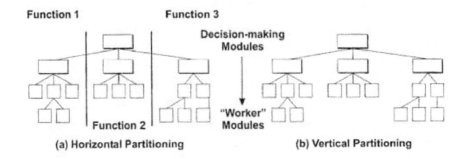

Horizontal and Vertical Partitioning

In **vertical partitioning**, the functionality is distributed among the modules--in a top-down manner. The modules at the top level called **control modules** perform the decision-making and do little processing whereas the modules at the low level called **worker modules** perform all input, computation and output tasks.

Concurrency

Computer has limited resources and they must be utilized efficiently as much as possible. To utilize these resources efficiently, multiple tasks must be executed concurrently. This requirement makes concurrency one of the major concepts of software design. Every system must be designed to allow multiple processes to execute concurrently, whenever possible. For example, if the current process is waiting for some event to occur, the system must execute some other process in the mean time.

However, concurrent execution of multiple processes sometimes may result in undesirable situations such as an inconsistent state, deadlock, etc. For example, consider two processes A and B and a data item Q1 with the value '200'. Further, suppose A and B are being executed concurrently and firstly A reads the value of Q1 (which is '200') to add '100' to it. However, before A updates es the value of Q1, B reads the value ofQ1 (which is still '200') to add '50' to it. In this situation, whether A or B first updates the value of Q1, the value of would definitely be wrong resulting in an inconsistent state of the system. This is because the actions of A and B are not synchronized with each other. Thus, the system must control the concurrent execution and synchronize the actions of concurrent processes.

One way to achieve synchronization is mutual exclusion, which ensures that two concurrent processes do not interfere with the actions of each other. To ensure this, mutual exclusion may use locking technique. In this technique, the processes need to lock the data item to be read or updated. The data item locked by some process cannot be accessed by other processes until it is unlocked. It implies that the process, that needs to access the data item locked by some other process, has to wait.

Developing a Design Model

To develop a complete specification of design (design model), four design models are needed. These models are listed below.

1. **Data design:** This specifies the data structures for implementing the software by converting data objects and their relationships identified during the analysis phase. Various studies suggest that design engineering should begin with data design, since this design lays the foundation for all other design models.

2. **Architectural design:** This specifies the relationship between the structural elements of the software, design patterns, architectural styles, and the factors affecting the ways in which architecture can be implemented.

3. **Component-level design:** This provides the detailed description of how structural elements of software will actually be implemented.

4. **Interface design:** This depicts how the software communicates with the system that interoperates with it and with the end-users.

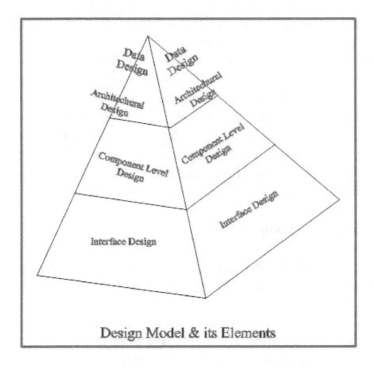

Design Model & its Elements

Introduction to design process

- The main aim of design engineering is to generate a model which shows firmness, delight and commodity.
- Software design is an iterative process through which requirements are translated into the blueprint for building the software.

Software quality guidelines

- A design is generated using the recognizable architectural styles and compose a good design characteristic of components and it is implemented in evolutionary manner for testing.

- A design of the software must be modular i.e the software must be logically partitioned into elements.
- In design, the representation of data , architecture, interface and components should be distinct.
- A design must carry appropriate data structure and recognizable data patterns.
- Design components must show the independent functional characteristic.
- A design creates an interface that reduce the complexity of connections between the components.
- A design must be derived using the repeatable method.
- The notations should be use in design which can effectively communicates its meaning.

Attributes of design

The attributes of design name as 'FURPS' are as follows:

Functionality:It evaluates the feature set and capabilities of the program.

Usability:It is accessed by considering the factors such as human factor, overall aesthetics, consistency and documentation.

Reliability: It is evaluated by measuring parameters like frequency and security of failure, output result accuracy, the mean-time-to-failure(MTTF), recovery from failure and the the program predictability.

Performance:It is measured by considering processing speed, response time, resource consumption, throughput and efficiency.

Supportability:

- It combines the ability to extend the program, adaptability, serviceability. These three term defines the maintainability.
- Testability, compatibility and configurability are the terms using which a system can be easily installed and found the problem easily.
- Supportability also consists of more attributes such as compatibility, extensibility, fault tolerance, modularity, reusability, robustness, security, portability, scalability.

Design concepts

The set of fundamental software design concepts are as follows:

1. Abstraction

- A solution is stated in large terms using the language of the problem environment at the highest level abstraction.
- The lower level of abstraction provides a more detail description of the solution.
- A sequence of instruction that contain a specific and limited function refers in a procedural abstraction.
- A collection of data that describes a data object is a data abstraction.

2. Architecture

- The complete structure of the software is known as software architecture.
- Structure provides conceptual integrity for a system in a number of ways.
- The architecture is the structure of program modules where they interact with each other in a specialized way.
- The components use the structure of data.
- The aim of the software design is to obtain an architectural framework of a system.
- The more detailed design activities are conducted from the framework.

3. Patterns

A design pattern describes a design structure and that structure solves a particular design problem in a specified content.

4. Modularity

- A software is separately divided into name and addressable components. Sometime they are called as modules which integrate to

satisfy the problem requirements.
- Modularity is the single attribute of a software that permits a program to be managed easily.

5. Information hiding
Modules must be specified and designed so that the information like algorithm and data presented in a module is not accessible for other modules not requiring that information.

6. Functional independence

- The functional independence is the concept of separation and related to the concept of modularity, abstraction and information hiding.
  - The functional independence is accessed using two criteria i.e Cohesion and coupling.

Cohesion

- Cohesion is an extension of the information hiding concept.
- A cohesive module performs a single task and it requires a small interaction with the other components in other parts of the program.

Coupling
Coupling is an indication of interconnection between modules in a structure of software.

7. Refinement

- Refinement is a top-down design approach.
  - It is a process of elaboration.
- A program is established for refining levels of procedural details.
- A hierarchy is established by decomposing a statement of function in a stepwise manner till the programming language statement are reached.

8. Refactoring

- It is a reorganization technique which simplifies the design of components without changing its function behaviour.
- Refactoring is the process of changing the software system in a way that it does not change the external behaviour of the code still improves its internal structure.

9. Design classes

- The model of software is defined as a set of design classes.
- Every class describes the elements of problem domain and that focus on features of the problem which are user visible.

Structure Charts

Structure Chart represent hierarchical structure of modules. It breaks down the entire system into lowest functional modules, describe functions and sub-functions of each module of a system to a greater detail. Structure Chart partitions the system into black boxes (functionality of the system is known to the users but inner details are unknown). Inputs are given to the black boxes and appropriate outputs are generated.

Modules at top level called modules at low level. Components are read from top to bottom and left to right. When a module calls another, it views the called module as black box, passing required parameters and receiving results.

Symbols used in construction of structured chart

Module
It represents the process or task of the system. It is of three types.

Control Module
A control module branches to more than one sub module.

Sub Module
Sub Module is a module which is the part (Child) of another module.

Library Module
Library Module are reusable and invokable from any module.

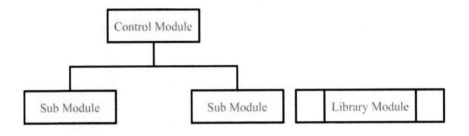

.

Conditional Call

It represents that control module can select any of the sub module on the basis of some condition.

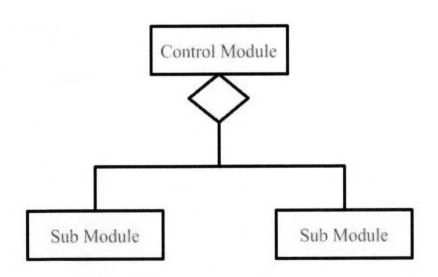

Loop (Repetitive call of module)
It represents the repetitive execution of module by the sub module.
A curved arrow represents loop in the module.

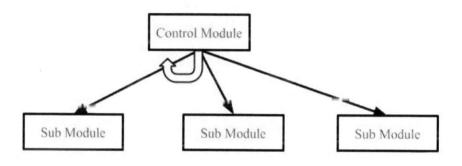

All the sub modules cover by the loop repeat execution of module.

Data Flow
It represents the flow of data between the modules. It is represented by
directed arrow with empty circle at the end.

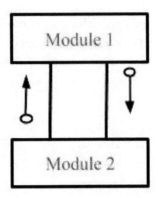

Control Flow

It represents the flow of control between the modules. It is represented by directed arrow with filled circle at the end.

Physical Storage

Physical Storage is that where all the information are to be stored.

Example : Structure chart for an Email server

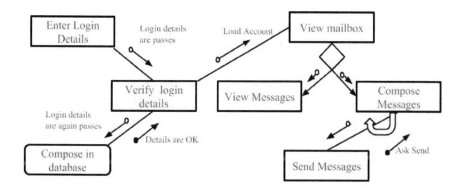

Types of Structure Chart:

1. **Transform Centered Structured:**

These type of structure chart are designed for the systems that receives an input which is transformed by a sequence of operations being carried out by one module.

2. **Transaction Centered Structure:**

These structure describes a system that processes a number of different types of transaction.

Structured Design

Structured design is a conceptualization of problem into several well-organized elements of solution. It is basically concerned with the solution design. Benefit of structured design is, it gives better understanding of how the problem is being solved. Structured design also makes it simpler for designer to concentrate on the problem more accurately.

Structured design is mostly based on 'divide and conquer' strategy where a problem is broken into several small problems and each small problem is individually solved until the whole problem is solved.

The small pieces of problem are solved by means of solution modules. Structured design emphasis that these modules be well organized in order to achieve precise solution.

These modules are arranged in hierarchy. They communicate with each other. A good structured design always follows some rules for communication among multiple modules, namely -

Cohesion - grouping of all functionally related elements.

Coupling - communication between different modules.

A good structured design has high cohesion and low coupling arrangements.

Function Oriented Design

In function-oriented design, the system is comprised of many smaller sub-systems known as functions. These functions are capable of performing significant task in the system. The system is considered as top view of all functions.

Function oriented design inherits some properties of structured design where divide and conquer methodology is used.

This design mechanism divides the whole system into smaller functions, which provides means of abstraction by concealing the information and their operation.. These functional modules can share information among themselves by means of information passing and using information available globally.

Another characteristic of functions is that when a program calls a function, the function changes the state of the program, which sometimes is not acceptable by other modules. Function oriented design works well where the system state does not matter and program/functions work on input rather than on a state.

Design Process

- The whole system is seen as how data flows in the system by means of data flow diagram.
- DFD depicts how functions changes data and state of entire system.
- The entire system is logically broken down into smaller units known as functions on the basis of their operation in the system.
- Each function is then described at large.

Object Oriented Design

Object oriented design works around the entities and their characteristics instead of functions involved in the software system. This design strategies focuses on entities and its characteristics. The whole concept of software solution revolves around the engaged entities.

Let us see the important concepts of Object Oriented Design:

- **Objects** - All entities involved in the solution design are known as objects. For example, person, banks, company and customers are treated as objects. Every entity has some attributes associated to it and has some methods to perform on the attributes.
- **Classes** - A class is a generalized description of an object. An object is an instance of a class. Class defines all the attributes, which an object can have and methods, which defines the functionality of the object.

In the solution design, attributes are stored as variables and functionalities are defined by means of methods or procedures.

- **Encapsulation** - In OOD, the attributes (data variables) and methods (operation on the data) are bundled together is called encapsulation. Encapsulation not only bundles important information of an object together, but also restricts access of the data and methods from the outside world. This is called information hiding.
- **Inheritance** - OOD allows similar classes to stack up in hierarchical manner where the lower or sub-classes can import, implement and re-use allowed variables and methods from their immediate super classes. This property of OOD is known as inheritance. This makes it easier to define specific class and to create generalized classes from specific ones.
- **Polymorphism** - OOD languages provide a mechanism where methods performing similar tasks but vary in arguments, can be assigned same name. This is called polymorphism, which allows a single interface performing tasks for different types. Depending upon how the function is invoked, respective portion of the code gets executed.

Design Process

Software design process can be perceived as series of well-defined steps. Though it varies according to design approach (function oriented or object oriented, yet It may have the following steps involved:

- A solution design is created from requirement or previous used system and/or system sequence diagram.
- Objects are identified and grouped into classes on behalf of similarity in attribute characteristics.
  - Class hierarchy and relation among them is defined.
    - Application framework is defined.

Software Design Approaches

Here are two generic approaches for software designing:

Top Down Design

We know that a system is composed of more than one sub-systems and it contains a number of components. Further, these sub-systems and components may have their on set of sub-system and components and creates hierarchical structure in the system.

Top-down design takes the whole software system as one entity and then decomposes it to achieve more than one sub-system or component based on some characteristics. Each sub-system or component is then treated as a system and decomposed further. This process keeps on running until the lowest level of system in the top-down hierarchy is achieved.

Top-down design starts with a generalized model of system and keeps on defining the more specific part of it. When all components are composed the whole system comes into existence.

Top-down design is more suitable when the software solution needs to be designed from scratch and specific details are unknown.

Bottom-up Design

The bottom up design model starts with most specific and basic components. It proceeds with composing higher level of components by using basic or lower level components. It keeps creating higher level components until the desired system is not evolved as one single component. With each higher level, the amount of abstraction is increased.

Bottom-up strategy is more suitable when a system needs to be created from some existing system, where the basic primitives can be used in the newer system.

Both, top-down and bottom-up approaches are not practical individually. Instead, a good combination of both is used.

CHAPTER SEVEN

METRICS

Metrics collection is an excellent way track the project, measure the performance. Software metrics provides objective information to help the project managers to do. The other set of metrics we would live to consider are known as Information Flow Metrics. The basis of information flow metrics is found upon the following concept the simplest system consists of the component, and it is the work that these components do and how they are fitted together that identify the complexity of the system. The following are the working definitions that are used in Information flow:

Component: Any element identified by decomposing a (software) system into it's constituent's parts.

Cohesion: The degree to which a component performs a single function.

Coupling: The term used to describe the degree of linkage between one component to others in the same system.

Information Flow metrics deal with this type of complexity by observing the flow of information among system components or modules. This metrics is given by **Henry and Kafura**. So it is also known as Henry and Kafura's Metric.

This metrics is based on the measurement of the information flow among system modules. It is sensitive to the complexity due to interconnection among system component. This measure includes the complexity of a software module is defined to be the sum of complexities of the procedures included in the module. A process contributes complexity due to the following two factors.

1. The complexity of the procedure code itself.
2. The complexity due to the procedure's connections to its environment. The effect of the first factor has been included through LOC (Line Of

Code) measure. For the quantification of the second factor, Henry and Kafura have defined two terms, namely FAN-IN and FAN-OUT.

FAN-IN: FAN-IN of a procedure is the number of local flows into that procedure plus the number of data structures from which this procedure retrieve information.

FAN -OUT: FAN-OUT is the number of local flows from that procedure plus the number of data structures which that procedure updates.

Procedure Complexity = Length * (FAN-IN * FANOUT)**2

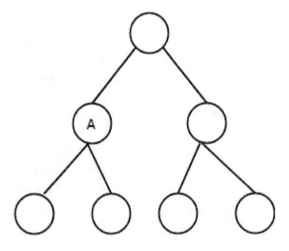

Fig: Aspects of Complexity

Benefits of Software Metrics and Measurements

- Metrics provides objective information throughout the software organization. This reduces the ambiguity that often surrounds complex and constrained software projects.
- Measurement helps managers to identify, prioritize, track and communicate project issues at all levels within the organization.
- Metrics can accurately describe the status of software project processes and products. It is key to objectively representing the progress of project activities and the quality of associated software products across the project life cycle. Metrics helps to answer questions such as "Is the project on schedule?" or "is the software ready to be delivered to the

user?" etc.

- Project metrics facilitates a proactive management strategy. Potential problems are objectively identified as risks to be assesses and managed. Existing problems can be better evaluated and prioritized. Metrics fosters the early discovery and correction of technical and management problems that can be more difficult or costly to resolve later.
- Software Project Managers can use metrics as a resource to anticipate problems and to avoid being forced into a reactive, fix \on fail approach.
- Metrics help the decision maker to assess the impacts of decisions objectively and make informed trade-offs to best meet project objectives and to optimize software project and product performance.
- Metrics provides an effective rationale for selecting the best alternatives. For example, the current software and IT business environments demand successful project performance. Business, technical and project managers must be able to defend the basis of their estimates and plans with historical performance data. Then, they must be able to justify changes to plans with current performance data.

Coding Standards and Guidelines

Different modules specified in the design document are coded in the Coding phase according to the module specification. The main goal of the coding phase is to code from the design document prepared after the design phase through a high-level language and then to unit test this code.

Good software development organizations want their programmers to maintain to some well-defined and standard style of coding called coding standards. They usually make their own coding standards and guidelines depending on what suits their organization best and based on the types of software they develop. It is very important for the programmers to maintain the coding standards otherwise the code will be rejected during code review.

Purpose of Having Coding Standards:

- A coding standard gives a uniform appearance to the codes written by different engineers.
- It improves readability, and maintainability of the code and it reduces complexity also.
  - It helps in code reuse and helps to detect error easily.
- It promotes sound programming practices and increases efficiency of the programmers.

Some of the coding standards are given below:

1. **Limited use of globals:**
These rules tell about which types of data that can be declared global and the data that can't be.

2. **Standard headers for different modules:**
For better understanding and maintenance of the code, the header of different modules should follow some standard format and information. The header format must contain below things that is being used in various companies:

- Name of the module
- Date of module creation
- Author of the module
- Modification history
- Synopsis of the module about what the module does
- Different functions supported in the module along with their input output parameters
- Global variables accessed or modified by the module

3. **Naming conventions for local variables, global variables, constants and functions:**

Some of the naming conventions are given below:

- Meaningful and understandable variables name helps anyone to understand the reason of using it.
- Local variables should be named using camel case lettering starting with small letter (e.g. **localData**) whereas Global variables names should start with a capital letter (e.g. **GlobalData**). Constant names should be formed using capital letters only (e.g. **CONSDATA**).
- It is better to avoid the use of digits in variable names.
- The names of the function should be written in camel case starting with small letters.
- The name of the function must describe the reason of using the function clearly and briefly.

4. **Indentation:**

Proper indentation is very important to increase the readability of the code. For making the code readable, programmers should use White spaces properly. Some of the spacing conventions are given below:

- There must be a space after giving a comma between two function arguments.
- Each nested block should be properly indented and spaced.
- Proper Indentation should be there at the beginning and at the end of each block in the program.

- All braces should start from a new line and the code following the end of braces also start from a new line.

5. **Error return values and exception handling conventions:**
All functions that encountering an error condition should either return a 0 or 1 for simplifying the debugging.

On the other hand, Coding guidelines give some general suggestions regarding the coding style that to be followed for the betterment of understandability and readability of the code. Some of the coding guidelines are given below :

6. **Avoid using a coding style that is too difficult to understand:**
Code should be easily understandable. The complex code makes maintenance and debugging difficult and expensive.

7. **Avoid using an identifier for multiple purposes:**
Each variable should be given a descriptive and meaningful name indicating the reason behind using it. This is not possible if an identifier is used for multiple purposes and thus it can lead to confusion to the reader. Moreover, it leads to more difficulty during future enhancements.

8. **Code should be well documented:**
The code should be properly commented for understanding easily. Comments regarding the statements increase the understandability of the code.

9. **Length of functions should not be very large:**
Lengthy functions are very difficult to understand. That's why functions should be small enough to carry out small work and lengthy

functions should be broken into small ones for completing small tasks.

10. Try not to use GOTO statement:

GOTO statement makes the program unstructured, thus it reduces the understandability of the program and also debugging becomes difficult.

- **Advantages of Coding Guidelines:**
- Coding guidelines increase the efficiency of the software and reduces the development time.
- Coding guidelines help in detecting errors in the early phases, so it helps to reduce the extra cost incurred by the software project.
- If coding guidelines are maintained properly, then the software code increases readability and understandability thus it reduces the complexity of the code.
- It reduces the hidden cost for developing the software.

Basic principles

This paper attempts to distill the large number of individual aphorisms on good software engineering into a small set of basic principles. Seven principles have been determined which form a reasonably independent and complete set. These are:

(1) manage using a phased life-cycle plan.

(2) perform continuous validation.

(3) maintain disciplined product control.

(4) use modern programming practices.

(5) maintain clear accountability for results.

(6) use better and fewer people.

(7) maintain a commitment to improve the process.

Code Verification Techniques

Code verification is the process used for checking the software code for errors introduced in the coding phase. The objective of code verification process is to check the software code in all aspects. This process includes checking the consistency of user requirements with the design phase. Note that code verification process does not concentrate on proving the correctness of programs. Instead, it verifies whether the software code has been translated according to the requirements of the user.

The code verification techniques are classified into two categories, namely, dynamic and static. The **dynamic technique** is performed by executing some test data. The outputs of the program are tested to find errors in the software code. This technique follows the conventional approach for testing the software code. In the **static technique,** the program is executed conceptually and without any data. In other words, the static technique does not use any traditional approach as used in the dynamic technique. Some of the commonly used static techniques are code reading, static analysis, symbolic execution, and code inspection and reviews.

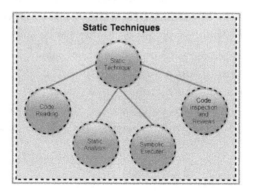

Code Reading

Code reading is a technique that concentrates on how to read and understand a computer program. It is essential for a software developer to know code reading. The process of reading a software program in order to understand it is known as **code reading or program reading.** In this process, attempts are made to understand the documents, software specifications, or software designs. The purpose of reading programs is to determine the correctness and consistency of the code. In addition, code reading is performed to enhance the software code without entirely changing the program or with minimal disruption in the current functionality of' the program. Code reading also aims at inspecting the code and removing (fixing) errors from it.

Code reading is a passive process and needs concentration. An effective code reading activity primarily focuses on reviewing 'what is important'. The general conventions that can be followed while reading the software code are listed below.

1. **Figure out what is important:** While reading the code, emphasis should be on finding graphical techniques (bold, italics) or positions (beginning or end of the section). Important comments may be highlighted in the introduction or at the end of the software code. The level of details should be according to the requirements of the software code.
2. **Read what is important:** Code reading should be done with the intent to check syntax and structure such as brackets, nested loops, and functions rather than the non-essentials such as name of the software developer who has written the software code.

Static Analysis

Static analysis comprises a set of methods used to analyze the source code or object code of the software to understand how the software functions and to set up criteria to check its correctness. Static analysis studies the source code without executing it and gives information about the structure of model used, data and control flows, syntactical accuracy, and much more. Due to this, there are several kinds of static analysis methods, which are listed below.

Control flow analysis: This examines the control structures (sequence, selection, and repetition) used in the code. It identifies incorrect and inefficient constructs and also reports unreachable code, that is, the code to which the control never reaches.

Data analysis: This ensures that-proper operations are applied to data objects (for example, data structures and linked lists). In addition, this method also ensures that the defined data is properly used. Data analysis comprises two methods, namely, data dependency and data-flow analysis. **Data dependency** (which determines the dependency of one variable on another) is essential for assessing the accuracy of synchronization across multiple processors. **Dataflow analysis** checks the definition and references of variables.

Fault/failure analysis: This analyzes the fault (incorrect model component) and failure (incorrect behaviour of a model component) in the model. This method uses input-output transformation descriptions to identify the conditions that are the cause for the failure. To determine the failures in certain conditions, the model design specification is checked.

Interface analysis: This verifies and validates the interactive and distributive simulations to check the software code. There are two basic techniques for the interface analysis, namely, model interface analysis and user interface analysis. **Model interface analysis** examines the sub-model interfaces and determines the accuracy of the interface structure. **User interface analysis** examines the user interface model and checks for precautionary steps taken to prevent errors during the user's interaction with the model'. This method also concentrates on how accurately the interface is integrated into. the overall model and simulation.

Symbolic Execution

Symbolic execution concentrates on assessing the accuracy of the model by using symbolic values instead of actual data values for input. Symbolic execution, also known as **symbolic evaluation,** is performed by providing symbolic inputs, which produce expressions for the output.

Symbolic execution uses a standard mathematical technique for representing the arbitrary program inputs (variables) in the form of symbols. To perform the calculation, a machine is employed to perform algebraic manipulation on the symbolic expressions. These expressions include symbolic data meant for execution. The symbolic execution is represented as a symbolic state symbol consisting of variable symbolic values, path, and the path conditions. The symbolic state for each step in the arbitrary input is updated. The steps that are commonly followed for updating the symbolic state considering all possible paths are listed below.

1. The read or the input symbol is created.
2. The assignment creates a symbolic value expression.
3. The conditions in symbolic state add constraints to the path condition.

The output of symbolic execution is represented in the form of a symbolic execution tree. The branches of the tree represent the paths of the model. There is a decision point to represent the nodes of the tree. This node is labeled with the symbolic values of the data at that junction. The leaves of the tree are complete paths through the model and they represent the output of symbolic execution. Symbolic execution helps in showing the correctness of the paths for all computations. Note that in this method the symbolic execution tree increases in size and creates complexity with growth in the model.

Code Inspection and Reviews

This technique is a formal and systematic examination of the source code to detect errors. During this process, the software is presented to the project managers and the users for a comment of approval. Before providing any comment, the inspection team checks the source code for errors. Generally, this team consists of the following.

1. **Moderator:** Conducts inspection meetings, checks errors-, and ensures that the inspection process is followed.
2. **Reader:** Paraphrases the operation of the software code.
3. **Recorder:** Keeps record of each error in the software code. This frees the task of other team members to think deeply about the software code.
4. **Author:** Observes the code inspection process silently and helps only when explicitly required. The role of the author is to understand the errors found in the software code.

As mentioned above, the reader paraphrases the meaning of small sections of code during the code inspection process. In other words, the reader translates the sections of code from a computer language to a commonly spoken language (such as English). The inspection process is carried out to check whether the implementation of the software code is done according to the user requirements. Generally, to conduct code inspections the following steps are performed.

1. **Planning:** After the code is compiled and there are no more errors and warning messages in the software code, the author submits the findings to the moderator who is responsible for forming the inspection team. After the inspection team is formed, the moderator distributes the listings as well as other related documents like design documentation to each team member. The moderator plans the inspection meetings and coordinates with the team members.
2. **Overview:** This is an optional step and is required only when the inspection team members are not aware of the functioning of the project. To familiarize the team members, the author provides details to make them understand the code.

3. **Preparation:** Each inspection team member individually examines the code and its related materials. They use a checklist to ensure that each problem area is checked. Each inspection team member keeps a copy of this checklist, in which all the problematic areas are mentioned.
4. **Inspection meeting:** This is carried out with all team members to review the software code. The moderator discusses the code under review with the inspection team members.

There are two checklists for recording the result of the code inspection, namely, code inspection checklist and inspection error list. **The code inspection checklist** contains a summary of all the errors of different types found in the software code. This checklist is used to understand the effectiveness of inspection process. **The inspection error list** provides the details of each error that requires rework. Note that this list contains details only of those errors that require the whole coding process to be repeated.

All errors in the checklist are classified as major or minor. An error is said to be major if it results in problems and later comes to the knowledge of the user. On the other hand, minor errors are spelling errors and non-compliance with standards. The classification of errors is useful when the software is to be delivered to the user and there is little time to review all the errors present in the software code.

At the conclusion of the inspection meeting, it is decided whether the code should be accepted in the current form or sent back for rework. In case the software code needs reworking, the author makes all the suggested corrections and then compiles the code. When the code becomes error-free, it is sent back to the moderator. The moderator checks the code that has been reworked. If the moderator is completely satisfied with the software code, inspection becomes formally complete and the process of testing the software code begins.

CHAPTER EIGHT

SOFTWARE TESTING

Static Testing is a type of a Software Testing method which is performed to check the defects in software without actually executing the code of the software application. Whereas in Dynamic Testing checks the code is executed to detect the defects.

Static testing is performed in early stage of development to avoid errors as it is easier to find sources of failures and it can be fixed easily. The errors that can't not be found using Dynamic Testing, can be easily found by Static Testing.

Static Testing Techniques:

There are mainly two type techniques used in Static Testing:

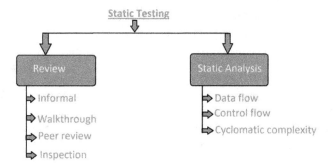

1. Review:

In static testing review is a process or technique that is performed to find the potential defects in the design of the software. It is process to detect and remove errors and defects in the different supporting documents like software requirements specifications. People examine the documents and sorted out errors, redundancies and ambiguities.

Review is of four types:

- **Informal:**
  In informal review the creator of the documents put the contents in front of audience and everyone gives their opinion and thus defects are identified in the early stage.
- **Walkthrough:**
  It is basically performed by experienced person or expert to check the defects so that there might not be problem further in the development or testing phase.
- **Peer review:**
  Peer review means checking documents of one-another to detect and fix the defects. It is basically done in a team of colleagues.
- **Inspection:**
  Inspection is basically the verification of document the higher authority like the verification of software requirement specifications (SRS).

2. **Static Analysis:**

Static Analysis includes the evaluation of the code quality that is written by developers. Different tools are used to do the analysis of the code and comparison of the same with the standard.

It also helps in following identification of following defects:

(a) Unused variables

(b) Dead code

(c) Infinite loops

(d) Variable with undefined value

(e) Wrong syntax

Static Analysis is of three types:

- **Data Flow:**
  Data flow is related to the stream processing.
- **Control Flow:**
  Control flow is basically how the statements or instructions are executed.

- **Cyclomatic Complexity:**
  Cyclomatic complexity is the measurement of the complexity of the program that is basically related to the number of independent paths in the control flow graph of the program.

Testing Fundamentals

Software testing is an investigation conducted to provide stakeholders with information about the quality of the product or service under test. Software testing can also provide an objective, independent view of the software to allow the business to appreciate and understand the risks of software implementation. In this video we descri the fundamentals of software testing.

Different types of Software Testing processes are described below:

- Unit Testing

It is a method by which individual units of source code are tested to determine if they are fit for use.

- Integration Testing

Here individual software modules are combined and tested as a group.

- Functionality Testing

It is a type of black box testing that bases its test cases on the specifications of the software component under test.

- Usability Testing

It is a technique used to evaluate a product by testing it on users.

- System Testing

It is testing conducted on a complete, integrated system to evaluate the system's compliance with its specified requirements.

- Performance Testing

It is testing that is performed, to determine how fast some aspect of a system performs under a particular workload.

- Load Testing

It refers to the practice of modeling the expected usage of a software program by simulating multiple users accessing the program concurrently.

Stress Testing

It is a form of testing that is used to determine the stability of a given system or entity

Black Box Testing

BLACK BOX TESTING, also known as Behavioral Testing, is a software testing method in which the internal structure/design/implementation of the item being tested is not known to the tester. These tests can be functional or non-functional, though usually functional.

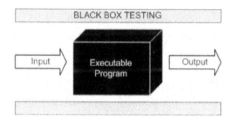

This method is named so because the software program, in the eyes of the tester, is like a black box; inside which one cannot see. This method attempts to find errors in the following categories:

- Incorrect or missing functions
- Interface errors
- Errors in data structures or external database access
- Behavior or performance errors
- Initialization and termination errors

Definition by ISTQB

- **black box testing:** Testing, either functional or non-functional, without reference to the internal structure of the component or system.

- **black box test design technique:** Procedure to derive and/or select test cases based on an analysis of the specification, either functional or non-functional, of a component or system without reference to its internal structure.

Example

A tester, without knowledge of the internal structures of a website, tests the web pages by using a browser; providing inputs (clicks, keystrokes) and verifying the outputs against the expected outcome.

Levels Applicable To

Black Box Testing method is applicable to the following levels of software testing:

- Integration Testing
- System Testing
- Acceptance Testing

The higher the level, and hence the bigger and more complex the box, the more black-box testing method comes into use.

Techniques

Following are some techniques that can be used for designing black box tests.

- *Equivalence Partitioning:* It is a software test design technique that involves dividing input values into valid and invalid partitions and

selecting representative values from each partition as test data.
- *Boundary Value Analysis:* It is a software test design technique that involves the determination of boundaries for input values and selecting values that are at the boundaries and just inside/ outside of the boundaries as test data.
- *Cause-Effect Graphing:* It is a software test design technique that involves identifying the cases (input conditions) and effects (output conditions), producing a Cause-Effect Graph, and generating test cases accordingly.

Advantages

- Tests are done from a user's point of view and will help in exposing discrepancies in the specifications.
- Tester need not know programming languages or how the software has been implemented.
- Tests can be conducted by a body independent from the developers, allowing for an objective perspective and the avoidance of developer-bias.
- Test cases can be designed as soon as the specifications are complete.

Disadvantages

- Only a small number of possible inputs can be tested and many program paths will be left untested.
- Without clear specifications, which is the situation in many projects, test cases will be difficult to design.
- Tests can be redundant if the software designer/developer has already run a test case.
- Ever wondered why a soothsayer closes the eyes when foretelling events? So is almost the case in Black Box Testing.

Boundary Value Analysis

Practically, due to time and budget considerations, it is not possible to perform exhausting testing for each set of test data, especially when there is a large pool of input combinations.

- We need an easy way or special techniques that can select test cases intelligently from the pool of test-case, such that all test scenarios are covered.
- We use two techniques - **Equivalence Partitioning & Boundary Value Analysis testing techniques** to achieve this.

Boundary Testing

Boundary testing is the process of testing between extreme ends or boundaries between partitions of the input values.

- So these extreme ends like Start- End, Lower- Upper, Maximum-Minimum, Just Inside-Just Outside values are called boundary values and the testing is called "boundary testing".
- The basic idea in boundary value testing is to select input variable values at their:

1. Minimum
2. Just above the minimum
3. A nominal value
4. Just below the maximum
5. Maximum

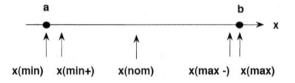

- In Boundary Testing, Equivalence Class Partitioning plays a good role
  - Boundary Testing comes after the Equivalence Class Partitioning.

Equivalent Class Partitioning

Equivalent Class Partitioning is a black box technique (code is not visible to tester) which can be applied to all levels of testing like unit, integration, system, etc. In this technique, you divide the set of test condition into a partition that can be considered the same.

- It divides the input data of software into different equivalence data classes.
- You can apply this technique, where there is a range in the input field.

Example 1: Equivalence and Boundary Value

- Let's consider the behavior of Order Pizza Text Box Below
- Pizza values 1 to 10 is considered valid. A success message is shown.
- While value 11 to 99 are considered invalid for order and an error message will appear, "Only 10 Pizza can be ordered"

Order Pizza:

Here is the test condition

1. Any Number greater than 10 entered in the Order Pizza field(let say 11) is considered invalid.
2. Any Number less than 1 that is 0 or below, then it is considered invalid.
3. Numbers 1 to 10 are considered valid
4. Any 3 Digit Number say -100 is invalid.

We cannot test all the possible values because if done, the number of test cases will be more than 100. To address this problem, we use equivalence partitioning hypothesis where we divide the possible values of tickets into groups or sets as shown below where the system behavior can be considered the same.

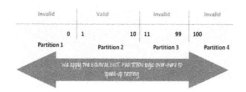

The divided sets are called Equivalence Partitions or Equivalence Classes. Then we pick only one value from each partition for testing. The hypothesis behind this technique is **that if one condition/value in a partition passes all others will also pass.** Likewise, if one condition in a **partition fails, all other conditions in that partition will fail.**

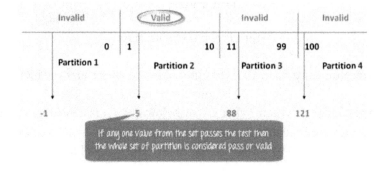

Boundary Value Analysis- in Boundary Value Analysis, you test boundaries between equivalence partitions

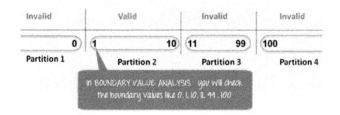

Cause-Effect Graph

Cause Effect Graph is a black box testing technique that graphically illustrates the relationship between a given outcome and all the factors that influence the outcome.

It is also known as Ishikawa diagram as it was invented by Kaoru Ishikawa or fish bone diagram because of the way it looks.

Cause Effect - Flow Diagram

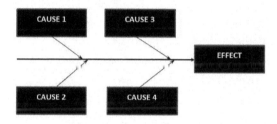

Circumstances - under which Cause-Effect Diagram used

- To Identify the possible root causes, the reasons for a specific effect, problem, or outcome.
- To Relate the interactions of the system among the factors affecting a particular process or effect.
- To Analyze the existing problems so that corrective action can be taken at the earliest.

Benefits :

- It Helps us to determine the root causes of a problem or quality using a structured approach.
- It Uses an orderly, easy-to-read format to diagram cause-and-effect relationships.
- It Indicates possible causes of variation in a process.
- It Identifies areas, where data should be collected for further study.
- It Encourages team participation and utilizes the team knowledge of the process.
- It Increases knowledge of the process by helping everyone to learn more about the factors at work and how they relate.

Steps for drawing cause-Effect Diagram:

- **Step 1 :** Identify and Define the Effect
- **Step 2 :** Fill in the Effect Box and Draw the Spine
- **Step 3:** Identify the main causes contributing to the effect being studied.
- **Step 4 :** For each major branch, identify other specific factors which may be the causes of the EFFECT.
- **Step 5 :** Categorize relative causes and provide detailed levels of causes.

White Box Testing

WHITE BOX TESTING (also known as Clear Box Testing, Open Box Testing, Glass Box Testing, Transparent Box Testing, Code-Based Testing or Structural Testing) is a software testing method in which the internal structure/design/implementation of the item being tested is known to the tester. The tester chooses inputs to exercise paths through the code and determines the appropriate outputs. Programming know-how and the implementation knowledge is essential. White box testing is testing beyond the user interface and into the nitty-gritty of a system.

This method is named so because the software program, in the eyes of the tester, is like a white/transparent box; inside which one clearly sees.

Definition by ISTQB

- **white box testing:** Testing based on an analysis of the internal structure of the component or system.
- **white-box test design technique:** Procedure to derive and/or select test cases based on an analysis of the internal structure of a component or system.

Example

A tester, usually a developer as well, studies the implementation code of a certain field on a webpage, determines all legal (valid and invalid) AND illegal inputs and verifies the outputs against the expected outcomes, which is also determined by studying the implementation code.

White Box Testing is like the work of a mechanic who examines the engine to see why the car is not moving.

Levels Applicable To

White Box Testing method is applicable to the following levels of software testing:

- Unit Testing: For testing paths within a unit.
- Integration Testing: For testing paths between units.
- System Testing: For testing paths between subsystems.

However, it is mainly applied to Unit Testing.

Advantages

- Testing can be commenced at an earlier stage. One need not wait for the GUI to be available.
- Testing is more thorough, with the possibility of covering most paths.

Disadvantages

- Since tests can be very complex, highly skilled resources are required, with a thorough knowledge of programming and implementation.
- Test script maintenance can be a burden if the implementation changes too frequently.
- Since this method of testing is closely tied to the application being tested, tools to cater to every kind of implementation/platform may not be readily available.

Data Flow Testing

Data flow testing is used to analyze the flow of data in the program. It is the process of collecting information about how the variables flow the data in the program. It tries to obtain particular information of each particular point in the process.

Data flow testing is a group of testing strategies to examine the control flow of programs in order to explore the sequence of variables according to the sequence of events. It mainly focuses on the points at which values assigned to the variables and the point at which these values are used by concentrating on both points, data flow can be tested.

Data flow testing uses the control flow graph to detect illogical things that can interrupt the flow of data. Anomalies in the flow of data are detected at the time of associations between values and variables due to:

- If the variables are used without initialization.
- If the initialized variables are not used at least once.

1. read x;
2. If(x>0)   (1, (2, t), x), (1, (2, f), x)
3. a= x+1   (1, 3, x)
4. if (x<=0) {   (1, (4, t), x), (1, (4, f), x)
5. if (x<1)   (1, (5, t), x), (1, (5, f), x)
6. x=x+1; (go to 5)   (1, 6, x)
else
7. a=x+1   (1, 7, x)
8. print a;   (6,(5, f)x), (6,(5,t)x)
                      (6, 6, x)
                      (3, 8, a), (7, 8, a).

In this code, we have a total 8 statements, and we will choose a path which covers all the 8 statements. As it is evident in the code, we cannot cover all the statements in a single path because if statement 2 is true then statements 4, 5, 6, 7 not covered, and if statement 4 is true then statement 2 and 3 are not covered.

So, we are taking two paths to cover all the statements.

1. x= 1

Path- 1, 2, 3, 8

Output = 2

When we set value of x as 1 first it come on step 1 to read and assign the value of x (we took 1 in path) then come on statement 2 (x>0 (we took 2 in path)) which is true and it comes on statement 3 (a= x+1 (we took 3 in path)) at last it comes on statement 8 to print the value of x (output is 2).

For the second path, we take the value of x is 1

2. Set x= -1

Path= 1, 2, 4, 5, 6, 5, 6, 5, 7, 8

Output = 2

When we set the value of x as ?1 then first, it comes on step 1 to read and assign the value of x (we took 1 in the path) then come on step number 2 which is false because x is not greater than 0 (x>0 and their x=-1). Due to false condition, it will not come on statement 3 and directly jump on statement 4 (we took 4 in path) and 4 is true (x<=0 and their x is less than 0) then come on statement 5 (x<1 (we took 5 in path)) which is also true so it will come on statement 6 (x=x+1 (we took 6 in path)) and here x is incremented by 1.

So,

$$x=-1+1$$

$$x=0$$

There is value of x become 0. Now it goes to statement 5(x<1 (we took 5 in path)) with value 0 and 0 is less than 1 so, it is true. Come on statement 6 (x=x+1 (we took 6 in path))

$$x=x+1$$

$$x=0+1$$

$$x=1$$

There x has become 1 and again goes to statement 5 (x<1 (we took 5 in path)) and now 1 is not less than 1 so, condition is false and it will come to else part means statement 7 (a=x+1 where the value of x is 1) and assign the value to a (a=2). At last, it come on statement 8 and print the value (Output is 2).

Make associations for the code:

Associations

In associations we list down all the definitions with all of its uses.

(1, (2, f), x), (1, (2, t), x), (1, 3, x), (1, (4, t), x), (1, (4, f), x), (1, (5, t), x), (1, (5, f), x), (1, 6, x), (1, 7, x), (6,(5, f)x), (6,(5,t)x), (6, 6, x), (3, 8, a), (7, 8, a).

How to make associations in data flow testing <link>

```
1 read x;
2 If(x>0)                    (1, (2, t), x), (1, (2, f), x)
3 a= x+1                     (1, 3, x)
4 if (x<=0) {                (1, (4, t), x), (1, (4, f), x)
5 if (x<1)                   (1, (5, t), x), (1, (5, f), x)
6 x=x+1; (go to 5)           (1, 6, x)
else
   7 a=x+1                   (1, 7, x)
   8 print a;                (6,(5, f)x), (6,(5,t)x)
                             (6, 6, x)
                             (3, 8, a), (7, 8, a).
```

- **(1, (2, t), x), (1, (2, f), x)**- This association is made with statement 1 (read x;) and statement 2 (If(x>0)) where x is defined at line number 1, and it is used at line number 2 so, x is the variable. Statement 2 is logical, and it can be true or false that's why the association is defined in two ways; one is (1, (2, t), x) for true and another is (1, (2, f), x) for false.
- **(1, 3, x)**- This association is made with statement 1 (read x;) and statement 3 (a= x+1) where x is defined in statement 1 and used in statement 3. It is a computation use.
- **(1, (4, t), x), (1, (4, f), x)**- This association is made with statement 1 (read x;) and statement 4 (If(x<=0)) where x is defined at line number 1 and it is used at line number 4 so x is the variable. Statement 4 is logical, and it can be true or false that's why the association is defined in two ways one is (1, (4, t), x) for true and another is (1, (4, f), x) for false.

- **(1, (5, t), x), (1, (5, f), x)**- This association is made with statement 1 (read x;) and statement 5 (if (x<1)) where x is defined at line number 1, and it is used at line number 5, so x is the variable. Statement 5 is logical, and it can be true or false that's why the association is defined in two ways; one is (1, (5, t), x) for true and another is (1, (5, f), x) for false.
- **(1, 6, x)**- This association is made with statement 1 (read x;) and statement 6 (x=x+1). x is defined in statement 1 and used in statement 6. It is a computation use.
- **(1, 7, x)**- This association is made with statement 1 (read x) and statement 7 (a=x+1). x is defined in statement 1 and used in statement 7 when statement 5 is false. It is a computation use.
- **(6, (5, f) x), (6, (5, t) x)**- This association is made with statement 6 (x=x+1;) and statement 5 if (x<1) because x is defined in statement 6 and used in statement 5. Statement 5 is logical, and it can be true or false that's why the association is defined in two ways one is (6, (5, f) x) for true and another is (6, (5, t) x) for false. It is a predicted use.
- **(6, 6, x)**- This association is made with statement 6 which is using the value of variable x and then defining the new value of x.

x=x+1

x= (-1+1)

Statement 6 is using the value of variable x that is ?1 and then defining new value of x [x= (-1+1) = 0] that is 0.
- **(3, 8, a)**- This association is made with statement 3(a= x+1) and statement 8 where variable a is defined in statement 3 and used in statement 8.
- **(7, 8, a)**- This association is made with statement 7(a=x+1) and statement 8 where variable a is defined in statement 7 and used in statement 8.

Definition, c-use, p-use, c-use some p-use coverage, p-use some c-use coverage in data flow testing <link>

The next task is to group all the associations in Definition, c-use, p-use, c-use some p-use coverage, p-use some c-use coverage categories.

See the code below:

```
1. read x;
2. If(x>0)                      (1, (2, t), x), (1, (2, f), x)
3. a= x+1                       (1, 3, x)
4. if (x<=0) {                  (1, (4, t), x), (1, (4, f), x)
5. if (x<1)                     (1, (5, t), x), (1, (5, f), x)
6. x=x+1; (go to 5)             (1, 6, x)
else
7. a=x+1                        (1, 7, x)
8. print a;                     (6,(5, f)x), (6,(5,t)x)
                                (6, 6, x)
```

So, these are the all association which contain definition, Predicate use (p-use), Computation use (c-use)

$(1, (2, f), x)$, $(1, (2, t), x)$, $(1, 3, x)$, $(1, (4, t), x)$, $(1, (4, f), x)$, $(1, (5, t), x)$, $(1, (5, f), x)$, $(1, 6, x)$, $(1, 7, x)$, $(6,(5, f)x)$, $(6,(5,t)x)$, $(6, 6, x)$, $(3, 8, a)$, $(7, 8, a)$, $(3, 8, a)$, $(7, 8, a)$

Definition

Definition of a variable is the occurrence of a variable when the value is bound to the variable. In the above code, the value gets bound in the first statement and then start to flow.

- If(x>0) is statement 2 in which value of x is bound with it.
  Association of statement 2 is (1, (2, f), x), (1, (2, t.)
  - a= x+1 is statement 3 bounded with the value of x
    Association of statement 3 is (1, 3, x)

All definitions coverage

(1, (2, f), x), (6, (5, f) x), (3, 8, a), (7, 8, a).

Predicate use (p-use)

If the value of a variable is used to decide an execution path is considered as predicate use (p-use). In control flow statements there are two

Statement 4 if (x<=0) is predicate use because it can be predicate as true or false. If it is true then if (x<1),6x=x+1; execution path will be executed otherwise, else path will be executed.

Computation use (c-use)

If the value of a variable is used to compute a value for output or for defining another variable.

Statement 3 a= x+1	(1, 3, x)
Statement 7 a=x+1	(1, 7, x)
Statement 8 print a	(3, 8, a), (7, 8, a).

These are **Computation use** because the value of x is used to compute and value of a is used for output.

All c-use coverage

(1, 3, x), (1, 6, x), (1, 7, x), (6, 6, x), (6, 7, x), (3, 8, a), (7, 8, a).

All c-use some p-use coverage

(1, 3, x), (1, 6, x), (1, 7, x), (6, 6, x), (6, 7, x), (3, 8, a), (7, 8, a).

All p-use some c-use coverage

(1, (2, f), x), (1, (2, t), x), (1, (4, t), x), (1, (4, f), x), (1, (5, t), x), (1, (5, f), x), (6, (5, f), x), (6, (5, t), x), (3, 8, a), (7, 8, a).

After collecting these groups, (By examining each point whether the variable is used at least once or not) tester can see all statements and variables are used. The statements and variables which are not used but exist in the code, get eliminated from the code.

Mutation Testing

Mutation Testing is a type of software testing where we mutate (change) certain statements in the source code and check if the test cases are able to find the errors. It is a type of White Box Testing which is mainly used for Unit Testing. The changes in mutant program are kept extremely small, so it does not affect the overall objective of the program.

The goal of Mutation Testing is to assess the quality of the test cases which should be robust enough to fail mutant code. This method is also called as Fault-based testing strategy as it involves creating a fault in the program

Mutation was originally proposed in 1971 but lost fervor due to the high costs involved. Now, again it has picked steam and is widely used for languages such as Java and XML.

- Execute Mutation Testing
- Types of Mutation Testing
- Mutation Score:
- Advantages of Mutation Testing:
- Disadvantages of Mutation Testing:

Execute Mutation Testing?

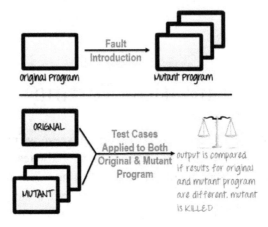

Fault Introduction

original Program → Mutant Program

ORIGINAL

MUTANT

Test Cases Applied to Both Original & Mutant Program

output is compared if results for original and mutant program are different, mutant is KILLED

Following are the steps to execute mutation testing(mutation analysis):

Step 1: Faults are introduced into the source code of the program by creating many versions called mutants. Each mutant should contain a single fault, and the goal is to cause the mutant version to fail which demonstrates the effectiveness of the test cases.

Step 2: Test cases are applied to the original program and also to the mutant program. A Test Case should be adequate, and it is tweaked to detect faults in a program.

Step 3: Compare the results of an original and mutant program.

Step 4: If the original program and mutant programs generate the different output, then that the mutant is killed by the test case. Hence the test case is good enough to detect the change between the original and the mutant program.

Step 5: If the original program and mutant program generate the same output, Mutant is kept alive. In such cases, more effective test cases need to be created that kill all mutants.

Types of Mutation Testing

In Software Engineering, Mutation testing could be fundamentally categorized into 3 types– statement mutation, decision mutation, and value mutation.

1. **Statement Mutation** - developer cut and pastes a part of a code of which the outcome may be a removal of some lines
2. **Value Mutation**- values of primary parameters are modified
3. **Decision Mutation**- control statements are to be changed

Mutation Score:

The mutation score is defined as the percentage of killed mutants with the total number of mutants.

- Mutation Score = (Killed Mutants / Total number of Mutants) * 100

Test cases are mutation adequate if the score is 100%. Experimental results have shown that mutation testing is an effective approach for measuring the adequacy of the test cases. But, the main drawback is that the high cost of generating the mutants and executing each test case against that mutant program.

Advantages of Mutation Testing:

Following are the advantages of Mutation Testing:

- It is a powerful approach to attain high coverage of the source program.

- This testing is capable comprehensively testing the mutant program.
- Mutation testing brings a good level of error detection to the software developer.
- This method uncovers ambiguities in the source code and has the capacity to detect all the faults in the program.
- Customers are benefited from this testing by getting a most reliable and stable system.

Disadvantages of Mutation Testing:

On the other side, the following are the disadvantages of Mutant testing:

- Mutation testing is extremely costly and time-consuming since there are many mutant programs that need to be generated.
- Since its time consuming, it's fair to say that this testing cannot be done without an automation tool.
- Each mutation will have the same number of test cases than that of the original program. So, a large number of mutant programs may need to be tested against the original test suite.
- As this method involves source code changes, it is not at all applicable for Black Box Testing.

Conclusion:

Do you want exhaustive testing of your application? The answer is Mutation testing. It is the most comprehensive technique to test a program. This is the method which checks for the effectiveness and accuracy of a testing program to detect the faults or errors in the system.

Levels of testing

A level of software testing is a process where every unit or component of a software/system is tested. The main goal of system testing is to evaluate the system's compliance with the specified needs.

There are many different testing levels which help to check behavior and performance for software testing. These testing levels are designed to recognize missing areas and reconciliation between the development lifecycle states. In SDLC models there are characterized phases such as requirement gathering, analysis, design, coding or execution, testing, and deployment.

All these phases go through the process of software testing levels. There are mainly four testing levels are:

1. Unit Testing
2. Integration Testing
3. System Testing
4. Acceptance Testing

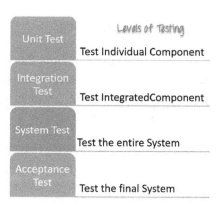

Each of these testing levels has a specific purpose. These testing level provide value to the software development lifecycle.

1) Unit testing:

A Unit is a smallest testable portion of system or application which can be compiled, liked, loaded, and executed. This kind of testing helps to test each module separately.

The aim is to test each part of the software by separating it. It checks that component are fulfilling functionalities or not. This kind of testing is performed by developers.

2) Integration testing:

Integration means combining. For Example, In this testing phase, different software modules are combined and tested as a group to make sure that integrated system is ready for system testing.

Integrating testing checks the data flow from one module to other modules. This kind of testing is performed by testers.

3) System testing:

System testing is performed on a complete, integrated system. It allows checking system's compliance as per the requirements. It tests the overall interaction of components. It involves load, performance, reliability and security testing.

System testing most often the final test to verify that the system meets the specification. It evaluates both functional and non-functional need for the testing.

4) Acceptance testing:

Acceptance testing is a test conducted to find if the requirements of a specification or contract are met as per its delivery. Acceptance testing is basically done by the user or customer. However, other stockholders can be involved in this process.

Other Types of Testing:

- Regression Testing
- Buddy Testing
- Alpha Testing
- Beta Testing

Conclusion:

- A level of software testing is a process where every unit or component of a software/system is tested.
- The primary goal of system testing is to evaluate the system's compliance with the specified needs.
- In Software Engineering, four main levels of testing are Unit Testing, Integration Testing, System Testing and Acceptance Testing.

Test Plan

A **TEST PLAN** is a document describing software testing scope and activities. It is the basis for formally testing any software/product in a project.

ISTQB Definition

- **test plan**: A document describing the scope, approach, resources and schedule of intended test activities. It identifies amongst others test items, the features to be tested, the testing tasks, who will do each task, degree of tester independence, the test environment, the test design techniques and entry and exit criteria to be used, and the rationale for their choice,and any risks requiring contingency planning. It is a record of the test planning process.
- **master test plan**: A test plan that typically addresses multiple test levels.
- **phase test plan**: A test plan that typically addresses one test phase.

Test Plan Types

One can have the following types of test plans:

- **Master Test Plan:** A single high-level test plan for a project/product that unifies all other test plans.
- **Testing Level Specific Test Plans:**Plans for each level of testing.

  - ◦ Unit Test Plan
  - ◦ Integration Test Plan
  - ◦ System Test Plan
  - ◦ Acceptance Test Plan

- **Testing Type Specific Test Plans:** Plans for major types of testing like Performance Test Plan and Security Test Plan.

Test Plan Template

The format and content of a software test plan vary depending on the processes, standards, and test management tools being implemented. Nevertheless, the following format, which is based on IEEE standard for software test documentation, provides a summary of what a test plan can/ should contain.

Test Plan Identifier:

- Provide a unique identifier for the document. (Adhere to the Configuration Management System if you have one.)

Introduction:

- Provide an overview of the test plan.
  - Specify the goals/objectives.
    - Specify any constraints.

References:

- List the related documents, with links to them if available, including the following:

  - Project Plan
  - Configuration Management Plan

Test Items:

- List the test items (software/products) and their versions.

Features to be Tested:

- List the features of the software/product to be tested.

- Provide references to the Requirements and/or Design specifications of the features to be tested

Features Not to Be Tested:

- List the features of the software/product which will not be tested.
  - Specify the reasons these features won't be tested.

Approach:

- Mention the overall approach to testing.
- Specify the testing levels [if it's a Master Test Plan], the testing types, and the testing methods [Manual/Automated; White Box/Black Box/ Gray Box]

Item Pass/Fail Criteria:

- Specify the criteria that will be used to determine whether each test item (software/product) has passed or failed testing.

Suspension Criteria and Resumption Requirements:

- Specify criteria to be used to suspend the testing activity.
- Specify testing activities which must be redone when testing is resumed.

Test Deliverables:

- List test deliverables, and links to them if available, including the following:
  - Test Plan (this document itself)
  - Test Cases
  - Test Scripts
  - Defect/Enhancement Logs

- ○ Test Reports

Test Environment:

- Specify the properties of test environment: hardware, software, network etc.
- List any testing or related tools.

Estimate:

- Provide a summary of test estimates (cost or effort) and/or provide a link to the detailed estimation.

Schedule:

- Provide a summary of the schedule, specifying key test milestones, and/or provide a link to the detailed schedule.

Staffing and Training Needs:

- Specify staffing needs by role and required skills.
- Identify training that is necessary to provide those skills, if not already acquired.

Responsibilities:

- List the responsibilities of each team/role/individual.

Risks:

- List the risks that have been identified.
- Specify the mitigation plan and the contingency plan for each risk.

Assumptions and Dependencies:

- List the assumptions that have been made during the preparation of this plan.
  - List the dependencies.

Approvals:

- Specify the names and roles of all persons who must approve the plan.
  - Provide space for signatures and dates. (If the document is to be printed.)

Test Plan Guidelines

- Make the plan concise. Avoid redundancy and superfluousness. If you think you do not need a section that has been mentioned in the template above, go ahead and delete that section in your test plan.
- Be specific. For example, when you specify an operating system as a property of a test environment, mention the OS Edition/Version as well, not just the OS Name.
  - Make use of lists and tables wherever possible. Avoid lengthy paragraphs.
- Have the test plan reviewed a number of times prior to baselining it or sending it for approval. The quality of your test plan speaks volumes about the quality of the testing you or your team is going to perform.
  - Update the plan as and when necessary. An out-dated and unused document stinks and is worse than not having the document in the first place.

A **Test case** is a document, which has a set of test data, preconditions, expected results and postconditions, developed for a particular test scenario in order to verify compliance against a specific requirement.

Test Case acts as the starting point for the test execution, and after applying a set of input values, the application has a definitive outcome and leaves the system at some end point or also known as execution postcondition.

Typical Test Case Parameters:

- Test Case ID
- Test Scenario
- Test Case Description
- Test Steps
- Prerequisite
- Test Data
- Expected Result
- Test Parameters
- Actual Result
- Environment Information
- Comments

Test Execution

Test execution is the process of executing the code and comparing the expected and actual results. Following factors are to be considered for a test execution process:

- Based on a risk, select a subset of test suite to be executed for this cycle.
- Assign the test cases in each test suite to testers for execution.
- Execute tests, report bugs, and capture test status continuously.
- Resolve blocking issues as they arise.
- Report status, adjust assignments, and reconsider plans and priorities daily.
- Report test cycle findings and status.

CHAPTER NINE

SOFTWARE MAINTENANCE

Software Maintenance is the process of modifying a software product after it has been delivered to the customer. The main purpose of software maintenance is to modify and update software application after delivery to correct faults and to improve performance.

Need for Maintenance –

Software Maintenance must be performed in order to:

- Correct faults.
- Improve the design.
- Implement enhancements.
- Interface with other systems.
- Accommodate programs so that different hardware, software, system features, and telecommunications facilities can be used.
- Migrate legacy software.
- Retire software.

Categories of Software Maintenance –

Maintenance can be divided into the following:

1. **Corrective maintenance:**
   Corrective maintenance of a software product may be essential either to rectify some bugs observed while the system is in use, or to enhance the performance of the system.

2. **Adaptive maintenance:**

   This includes modifications and updations when the customers need the product to run on new platforms, on new operating systems, or when they need the product to interface with new hardware and software.

3. **Perfective maintenance:**

   A software product needs maintenance to support the new features that the users want or to change different types of functionalities of the system according to the customer demands.

4. **Preventive maintenance:**

   This type of maintenance includes modifications and updations to prevent future problems of the software. It goals to attend problems, which are not significant at this moment but may cause serious issues in future.

Reverse Engineering –

Reverse Engineering is processes of extracting knowledge or design information from anything man-made and reproducing it based on extracted information. It is also called back Engineering.

Software Reverse Engineering –

Software Reverse Engineering is the process of recovering the design and the requirements specification of a product from an analysis of it's code. Reverse Engineering is becoming important, since several existing software products, lack proper documentation, are highly unstructured, or their structure has degraded through a series of maintenance efforts.

Why Reverse Engineering?

- Providing proper system documentatiuon.
- Recovery of lost information.
- Assisting with maintenance.
- Facility of software reuse.
- Discovering unexpected flaws or faults.

Used of Software Reverse Engineering –

- Software Reverse Engineering is used in software design, reverse engineering enables the developer or programmer to add new features to the existing software with or without knowing the source code.

- Reverse engineering is also useful in software testing, it helps the testers to study the virus and other malware code .

Benefits of Software Application Maintenance

Performance Improvement

Majority of the software maintenance programs will include up gradation of the program. A maintenance program for software entitles the user to a full year of free upgrades the upgrades are designed in order to address and fix issues encountered by users of the application. These upgrades improve the overall performance and functionality of the application. Moreover, they enable the software to last longer by increasing its life cycle.

Fixes Various Bugs

The software maintenance packages that are provided by the vendors at the time of software purchase keep you covered from all the bugs and various software issues. Since they are in a warranty period for a particular time period, these fixes are free of cost. However, post expiration of the warranty period, the owner needs to shell out the maintenance charges from one's own pocket.

Up To Date With Current Trends

Technology and the business depended on technology are the two most fast paced aspects that change on an everyday basis. Therefore, in order to keep your business in line with the recent technologies, it gets necessary to keep your software apps updated. This is exactly what the software application maintenance does. It keeps you in pace with the present technological trends and make sure that your organization gets to leverage all the benefits of the new technologies.

No Need To Spend Extra Bucks

The last but not the least benefit is from the financial point of view. The software maintenance programs enable the users to maintain a control over their expenditure on the software. Since every software maintenance program keeps the users covered for a period of nearly one year, it reduces the investment of an organization for its IT department to a huge extent. In case you are using cloud-based applications, the maintenance fee is usually included in the monthly charges that a user pays for the services.

Types of maintenance

There are four types of maintenance, namely, corrective, adaptive, perfective, and preventive. Corrective maintenance is concerned with fixing errors that are observed when the software is in use. Adaptive maintenance is concerned with the change in the software that takes place to make the software adaptable to new environment such as to run the software on a new operating system. Perfective maintenance is concerned with the change in the software that occurs while adding new functionalities in the software. Preventive maintenance involves implementing changes to prevent the occurrence of errors. The distribution of types of maintenance by type and by percentage of time consumed.

Corrective maintenance deals with the repair of faults or defects found in day-today system functions. A defect can result due to errors in software design, logic and coding. Design errors occur when changes made to the software are incorrect, incomplete, wrongly communicated, or the change request is misunderstood. Logical errors result from invalid tests and conclusions, incorrect implementation of design specifications, faulty logic flow, or incomplete test of data. All these errors, referred to as residual errors, prevent the software from conforming to its agreed specifications. Note that the need for corrective maintenance is usually initiated by bug reports drawn by the users.

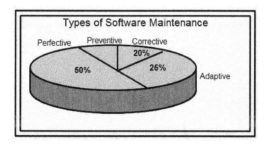

In the event of a system failure due to an error, actions are taken to restore the operation of the software system. The approach in corrective maintenance is to locate the original specifications in order to determine what the system was originally designed to do. However, due to pressure from management, the maintenance team sometimes resorts to emergency fixes known as patching. Corrective maintenance accounts for 20% of all the maintenance activities.

Adaptive Maintenance

Adaptive maintenance is the implementation of changes in a part of the system, which has been affected by a change that occurred in some other part of the system. Adaptive maintenance consists of adapting software to changes in the environment such as the hardware or the operating system. The term environment in this context refers to the conditions and the influences which act (from outside) on the system. For example, business rules, work patterns, and government policies have a significant impact on the software system.

For instance, a government policy to use a single 'European currency' will have a significant effect on the software system. An acceptance of this change will require banks in various member countries to make significant changes in their software systems to accommodate this currency. Adaptive maintenance accounts for 25% of all the maintenance activities.

Perfective Maintenance

Perfective maintenance mainly deals with implementing new or changed user requirements. Perfective maintenance involves making functional enhancements to the system in addition to the activities to increase the system's performance even when the changes have not been suggested by faults. This includes enhancing both the function and efficiency of the code and changing the functionalities of the system as per the users' changing needs.

Examples of perfective maintenance include modifying the payroll program to incorporate a new union settlement and adding a new report in the sales analysis system. Perfective maintenance accounts for 50%, that is, the largest of all the maintenance activities.

Preventive Maintenance

Preventive maintenance involves performing activities to prevent the occurrence of errors. It tends to reduce the software complexity thereby improving program understandability and increasing software maintainability. It comprises documentation updating, code optimization, and code restructuring. Documentation updating involves modifying the documents affected by the changes in order to correspond to the present state of the system. Code optimization involves modifying the programs for faster execution or efficient use of storage space. Code restructuring involves transforming the program structure for reducing the complexity in source code and making it easier to understand.

Preventive maintenance is limited to the maintenance organization only and no external requests are acquired for this type of maintenance. Preventive maintenance accounts for only 5% of all the maintenance activities.

Software Reliability Models

- A software reliability model indicates the form of a random process that defines the behavior of software failures to time.
- Software reliability models have appeared as people try to understand the features of how and why software fails, and attempt to quantify software reliability.
- Over 200 models have been established since the early 1970s, but how to quantify software reliability remains mostly unsolved.
  - There is no individual model that can be used in all situations. No model is complete or even representative.
    - Most software models contain the following parts:
      - Assumptions
      - Factors
- A mathematical function that includes the reliability with the elements. The mathematical function is generally higher-order exponential or logarithmic.

Reliability Modeling Techniques

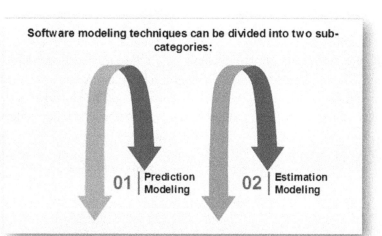

Software modeling techniques can be divided into two sub-categories:

01 | Prediction Modeling

02 | Estimation Modeling

SOFTWARE RELIABILITY MODELS

ISSUES	PREDICTION MODELS	ESTIMATION MODELS
DATA REFERENCE	Uses historical data	Uses data from the current software development effort
WHEN USED IN DEVELOPMENT CYCLE	Usually made prior to development or test phases; can be used as early as concept phase	Usually made later in life cycle(after some data have been collected); not typically used in concept or development phases
TIME FRAME	Predict reliability at some future time	Estimate reliability at either present or some future time

Reliability Models

A reliability growth model is a numerical model of software reliability, which predicts how software reliability should improve over time as errors are discovered and repaired. These models help the manager in deciding how much efforts should be devoted to testing. The objective of the project manager is to test and debug the system until the required level of reliability is reached.

Following are the Software Reliability Models are:

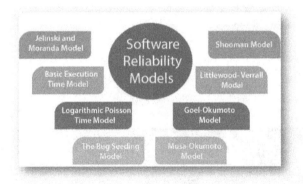

Reliability Testing

Software reliability testing a testing technique that relates to testing a software's ability to function given environmental conditions consistently that helps uncover issues in the software design and functionality.

Parameters involved in Reliability Testing:

Dependent elements of reliability Testing:

- Probability of failure-free operation
- Length of time of failure-free operation
- The environment in which it is executed

Key Parameters that are measured as part of reliability are given below:

- MTTF: Mean Time To Failure
- MTTR: Mean Time To Repair
- MTBF: Mean Time Between Failures (= MTTF + MTTR)

~

Important Questions

- What is meant by software development life cycle ? Discuss different phases of development life cycle in brief .
- Define software process. Elaborate on various characteristics of software process.
- List the major attributes of good quality software explain cyclomatic metric complexity matrix in detail
- What is the need for SRS ? Give a significant components of SRS .
- Give the design principles and explain in brief about the structured design methodology.
- What are the various method for code verification and give a few guidelines for good code
- How problem domain is pecified in Software Engineering ? Also explain various Software Engineering challenges.
- What is structured design methodology pxplain in detail.
- Define Metrics. Explain any two Software of design metrics.
- Explain various Programming principle to be implemented develop system code.
- Explain "Code inspections" and "Static analysis" techniques for Code-verification.
- Define Software testing. Also explain its various software Testing .

Thank You

This book was intended to aid students on their path to knowledge. May we continue to gain knowledge,as wel as pass on our knowledge to future generations

Notes

www.ingramcontent.com/pod-product-compliance
Lightning Source LLC
Chambersburg PA
CBHW071110050326
40690CB00008B/1172